Crusoes in Siberia
by Tivadar Soros

Crusoes in Siberia

by
Tivadar Soros
(Dr. Teodoro Schwartz)

Prefaces by Paul Soros and George Soros,
Introduction by Humphrey Tonkin

The Fairest Judgment
A Tale by Tivadar Soros
(Teo Melas)

Translated from Esperanto and Edited
by Humphrey Tonkin

Mondial

Mondial
New York

Tivadar Soros (Teodoro Ŝvarc, Teodoro Schwartz, Teo Melas):
Crusoes in Siberia
and
The Fairest Judgment
Translated from Esperanto and edited by Humphrey Tonkin

Original titles in Esperanto:
Modernaj Robinzonoj: En la siberia praarbaro
(Literatura Mondo, 1923/1924)
La plej justa juĝo (Literatura Mondo, 1/1 [October 1922]: 5-6)

Copyright © 2011 Paul and George Soros.
Translation, Translator's Introduction, Notes
© 1998, 2010 Humphrey Tonkin.

Illustrations and maps: Literatura Mondo, Archives of the editor, Literary Digest, Mondial, Yale University Library;
Map 1 is published by permission of Winfried Dallmann of the Norwegian Polar Institute.

ISBN 9781595692184 (paperback)
9781595691828 (hardcover)
9781595692054 (eBook editions)
B004F9P7X2 (Amazon Kindle, ASIN)

All rights reserved. No part of this book shall be reproduced or transmitted in any form or by any means, electronic, mechanical, magnetic, photographic including photocopying, recording or by any information storage and retrieval system, without prior written permission of the publisher, the translator, or the estate of the author.

2011, Mondial, New York
www.mondialbooks.com

Contents

Preface by George Soros ... i
Preface by Paul Soros ... iv

Translator's Introduction (Humphrey Tonkin) ... ix
Notes on the Translation ... xxiv
Illustrations ... xxv

Crusoes in Siberia ... 1

Introduction ... 3

I Captivity ... 5
In which our kind reader is informed of the pleasures of prisoners of war, of the humane conduct of warring parties and of something that allows the continuation of this story.

II Escape ... 11
In which the reader discovers that it is not enough simply to decide to escape.

III Consultation ... 17
In this chapter the reader learns that it is no simple matter to travel through virgin forest.

IV Choice ... 22
Wherein are described a few of the characters with whom we will live, or, in some cases, die.

V First Obstacles ... 27
In this chapter the author shows how continued progress, like most things in life, takes longer than expected.

VI The Crossing ... 31
*Here the reader will learn about efforts so great
that they might move mountains.*

VII Pursuit ... 36
*This chapter shows that being the object of hostile pursuit
sometimes has its agreeable side.*

VIII Among the Orochen ... 41
*The reader learns that there are savages not only in Europe
but also in Eastern Siberia.*

IX A Visit to an Orochen Village ... 45
*The reader with no interest in Orochen villages need not read this chapter,
in which the author describes certain characteristics of the nomadic life.*

X In the Forest ... 49
*If the reader is interested, he can read in this chapter about
the so-called "virgin forest."*

XI On the Vitim ... 54
*So far, our adventurous way has taken us by land, but now we continue
by river. After many difficulties we finally reach our Eldorado.*

Appendix 1: Who are the Orochen? ... 61
Appendix 2: Maps ... 66
Notes ... 77

The Fairest Judgment ... 89

Preface by George Soros

This book is my father's account of his adventures in the First World War when he led a breakout from a prisoner of war camp in Siberia. It is a companion piece to *Masquerade*, my father's account of his family's adventures during the German occupation of Hungary in the Second World War. These two episodes in my father's life are closely connected. His adventures in the First World War prepared him for what was to come in the Second. He learned that there are extraordinary times when the normal rules don't apply and one must be prepared to break the rules in order to survive. Clinging to property or insisting on comfortable living conditions can have fatal consequences. When he joined the army as a volunteer, he was an ambitious young man, but after his experiences in the Russian Revolution he gave up his ambitions. He was more concerned with living his life the right way than amassing material wealth. Money was only a means to an end, not an end in itself. He saw the limitations of bourgeois values and developed his own value system.

He passed on his values to my brother and me and those values have guided me ever since. This may sound strange coming from a man who has amassed an immense fortune but the fact is that I have never been interested in money for its own sake; otherwise I could never have given away so much of it. As a schoolboy, I used to join my father in the swimming pool after school and after swimming he would regale me with an installment of his adventures. In this way they became an important part of my childhood. They helped to prepare me for my own adventures in the Second World War. The German occupation of Hungary became the formative experience of my life and it turned out to have a very positive influence on my outlook on life. It taught me how to handle risk. My father was well prepared. He immediately recognized that this was one of those extraordinary occasions which require extraordinary measures. He arranged for false identities for his family and he also helped many other people. The story is accurately recounted by my father in *Masquerade*.

Here I want to mention only one episode in my life which was directly affected by my father's experiences during the Russian Revolution. I am referring to when I established a foundation in what was then the Soviet Union. During the early days of Glasnost when Gorbachev called Sakharov in Gorky and asked him to resume his patriotic activities in Moscow I immediately realized that something had changed in the Soviet regime. If it had been business as usual, Sakharov might have been allowed to emigrate, but not to return to Moscow. This prompted me to go to Moscow as soon as I could and try to replicate what I had done in my native Hungary by setting up a foundation with local participation. I was guided by my father's experiences in the Russian Revolution. He had told me that in revolutionary times the impossible becomes possible. He who sits down first at a desk abandoned by the director of an institution can take over his role. Other foundations sought legal authorization and it took them several years to obtain it because authorities were not functioning properly. We started operating without permission and we stole a march on the others. For a couple of years we were the only game in town. I felt at home in Russia. After all, we were old acquaintances. I had lived through the Russian Revolution through my father.

The story my father tells in this book represents only a fraction of his experiences during the Russian Revolution. It was published in the first volume of *Literatura Mondo*, the principal Esperanto literary magazine of the day, which he founded and owned. I believe that he intended to publish additional articles just as he told his story to me in the swimming pool in installments, but he did not follow through.

The only other article of his in *Literatura Mondo* is a story about a beautiful girl in an Indian village. I don't know whether my father invented the story or not, but it is characteristic enough of his sense of humor that we have included it in the book as an appendix.

Preface by Paul Soros

I was around eleven years old when I heard from my father the story described in this book. There are a couple of stories that he told me relating to the same period. One had to do with how he received the Austro-Hungarian equivalent of the Iron Cross, the name I no longer recall. He was a lieutenant and was told to send a sentry about 50 feet ahead of the ditch they were dug in to observe the status of the Russian ditch opposite. He asked for a volunteer. One of the soldiers volunteered, crawled out around 30 feet when he was shot. He asked for another volunteer to bring him back. Silence. He heard himself say "what's the matter guys, do you expect me to go to get him?" Silence. He realized it was a stupid thing to make a threat that he did not mean and put himself in an impossible situation but he couldn't undo it and had no choice but to crawl out himself. Luckily, he was not shot.

The other anecdote had to do with his arrival in a prisoner-of-war camp in Siberia in 1915. There were barrels of caviar. Everybody gorged themselves on caviar – breakfast, lunch and dinner. After three weeks nobody wanted to look at caviar much less eat it.

At the prisoner-of-war camp he was elected trustee representing the officers. Word came around that when control of a neighboring war prisoner camp switched from the Whites to the Reds, the officers' trustees were shot. This prompted him to organize the episode described in this book.

Eventually he managed to reach Moscow. He and his friend went to the local tribunal looking for work. His friend went in first to see the chief judge of the tribunal and addressed the chief judge as "tovarish" (comrade). The chief judge sent him to shovel coal in the cellar. When my father heard this, he addressed the chief judge as "gospodin" (sir) and was put on the bench. The only other thing that I remember is that he was involved in the Esperanto movement and he saw Chaliapin sing Boris Gudonov in the opera.

Unfortunately, the Bolshevik government would not allow repatriation of Hungarian officers. The reason was that after the war there was a brief period of Bolshevik rule in Hungary which was suppressed by a counter-revolution. The Reds in Russia were holding the Hungarian officers as hostages to secure the survival of the Reds imprisoned in Hungary. It was only in 1921, assuming the false identity of an Austrian officer that he was able to leave Russia and return to Hungary.

According to my mother he returned to Hungary a changed man. When he enlisted in 1914 he was an ambitious young lawyer, the first in his family to go to University. The experiences and survival of those years of turmoil in Russia were the formative influences in his life, making him a man with his own value system, with an unconventional outlook, without the conventional ambitions, appreciating life in all its variety and wishing to make the most of it in terms of what he considered interesting and important.

As his book describes only a brief episode, here is a thumbnail sketch of how his life turned out to be. After his return he married my mother and edited and published *Literatura Mondo*, an Esperanto magazine. It sold around the world, including countries with hard currencies, at a time when local currencies in Central Europe were worthless. Combined with funds from my mother's family, the proceeds allowed him to invest in apartment buildings in Budapest, Vienna and Berlin at a fraction of their replacement value, on the theory that when life returns to normal, the value of good apartment buildings will be in line with their cost of construction. Indeed, that turned out to be the case and he was assured of a comfortable life without being in the rat race. As he was not interested in amassing a fortune, he didn't let work interfere with making the most of life. His office hours were 10 – 12, occasionally also from 4 – 5. He picked us up after school at 12 or 1 p.m. and we went swimming, skating or skiing depending on the season. In the afternoon he went to a coffeehouse to read the domestic and foreign papers as he had a keen interest in political developments around the world. Christmas vacations we went skiing in Austria or Switzerland and the summers he spent at our summer house on an island in the Danube north of Budapest. In addition, he traveled extensively on his own, to satisfy his curiosity, including two trips to the U.S. and to the Soviet Union, which was far from customary for people in Central Europe in the thirties.

Actually my father was a very good lawyer. He had three paying clients, a stock-broker cum investment banker, a very rich landowning family and the business partner of my retired grandfather. The rest of his practice was semi pro bono, dealing with the legal problems of poor acquaintances who turned to him for help. The reason I can say he must have been a very good lawyer is that he explained to me that when a conflict goes to court it is the costliest and worst outcome for both parties and it is a failure of one or both of the lawyers who put their own ego and greed ahead of their client's best interests. As he was not interested in becoming wealthy he could afford to act accordingly.

When Germany occupied Hungary in March 1944, the existence of Auschwitz was not known at the time, but within three days my father predicted that anyone of a Jewish background would be in mortal danger and before the start of any persecution had decided that the family will have to break up, with everyone living separately under a false identity, so that if one got into trouble he didn't endanger the others. A book called *Masquerade* written by my father many years later describes our family history from March 1944 till the end of the war.

This was my father's finest hour, as later under the persecutions he kept his cool and was able to help numerous people that he knew from his normal life, but typically was smart enough to meet them in public spaces so that nobody knew his new name, address or phone number. It was certainly due to his foresight, judgment and guidance that we as a family survived this period.

The best capital is in your capital (pun intended). This was a saying of my father and it certainly applied to the vicissitudes of the post-war era in Hungary.

After the Russian occupation of Budapest I was taken as a military-age young man a prisoner of war by the Russians, but was able to escape while in transit. To provide some diplomatic protection, my father, who spoke fluent Russian, became legal counsel to the Swiss Embassy who then represented the U.S. in Hungary.

In 1947 when after Czechoslovakia the Communists took over in Hungary, my father told my younger brother George, who was 17 at the time and in school in England, not to come home even though it was no longer possible to send him money from Communist Hungary.

At the end of 1947, I was able to get out of Hungary as a member of the Olympic Ski Team to the winter Olympics in St. Moritz, Switzerland, and I defected. As a consequence, my father was disbarred. It was the practice of the Stalinist regime in Hungary to exile "class enemies" from Budapest, confiscating their apartments and forcing them to share the homes of former small landowners, so-called "kulaks," in the country, making life for both "class enemies" miserable.

The Russian political influence was managed out of the Russian embassy, but the Russian occupying army had a special Commendatura that had to contract for supplies, lease property, etc. So my father became their lawyer, which protected him from the edicts of the local Communists.

At the end of the '56 Revolution, there was a two-week window before the Iron Curtain was re-established so my parents were able to escape and come to America. My father was able to indulge his old interest in travel in the U.S. and abroad. He died of cancer at age 75.

I and my brother consider it to be our good fortune to grow up observing how our father lived and dealt with the problems of the world.

Translator's Introduction

I

"We have succeeded in convincing our editor-in-chief, whose first principle in that role is not to publish anything in the magazine written by himself, that our readers might be interested in knowing more about him. Accordingly, with a gesture of resigned acquiescence, he has passed on to us the manuscript that won him a prize at the International Floral Games in Manresa and that has been commended by the Esperantist Literary Association. His comment: 'Take it, but the responsibility is yours!' We hope that our readers, when they have read the interesting adventures of Dr. Teo Schwartz, will not find us too hasty, since we assumed this responsibility with enthusiasm."

With these words, the June 1923 issue of the Esperanto magazine *Literatura Mondo* began the serialization of *Modernaj Robinzonoj*, the slim volume of wartime recollections written in Esperanto by the young Teodoro Schwartz, who later became known in other circles as Tivadar Soros. Seven monthly installments appeared in all, the last published in the December 1923 issue; and in February of the following year the magazine already carried an advertisement announcing the publication of the complete text [Figure 4].[1]

---

1 The little book, when it finally appeared, actually bore two dates and two publishers: the cover [Figure 5] announced that it was a publication of Literatura Mondo and carried the date 1924, while the title page [Figure 6] gave "Globus Presartinstituto Akcia Societo" as the publisher and the date 1923. Globus Institute of Printing Arts was the printer of the magazine *Literatura Mondo* and the volumes published under the Literatura Mondo name, so the title page may simply represent confusion of printer and publisher or may indicate that originally Soros contracted with Globus for a kind of private printing, bringing the little book under the umbrella of Literatura Mondo shortly before it was actually published.

Soros was some 28 years old when, shortly after his return from military captivity in Siberia, he and several of his Esperanto-speaking friends launched the literary journal *Literatura Mondo* and the publishing operation of the same name. The first issue of the journal bore the date October 1922 [Figure 1]. The International Language Esperanto had first seen the light of day in 1887 and, while *Literatura Mondo* was by no means the earliest literary magazine in the language, it was arguably the most influential. Two other founders of the enterprise, the young medical doctor Kálmán Kalocsay and the actor Gyula Baghy, were to become widely recognized as leaders of a so-called Budapest School of poets, novelists and commentators on the language, who brought Esperanto literature to maturity over the next ten or fifteen years. Kalocsay was mentor to many aspiring writers, and he himself published several highly influential volumes of poetry, original and translated, and numerous contributions to the stylistics and linguistics of Esperanto. Baghy, like Soros, was also a recent returnee from military captivity in Siberia: he was captured in September 1915 and remained imprisoned in a succession of camps in Siberia and Manchuria until his return to Budapest on December 23, 1920. A prolific writer of poetry, drama, and fiction, he published two fictionalized accounts of his Siberian captivity, *Viktimoj* (Victims, 1925) and *Sur sanga tero* (On Bloody Ground, 1933), the former also serialized in *Literatura Mondo*.

The team of Soros, Kalocsay and Baghy was extraordinary by any measure. All three were optimistically convinced of their own capabilities; all three were massively talented in different ways; and all three had a kind of infectious enthusiasm for their various undertakings. When, for the World Esperanto Congress in Nuremberg in 1923, they teamed up to present a cabaret, their performance was, according to fellow-Esperantist and historian Edmond Privat, "a veritable feast of good taste and linguistic brilliance." The August 1923 issue of *Literatura Mondo* reports wryly on their triumphs: "Although for various reasons the material side of our enterprise was not so propitious that we could through this means strengthen the financial base of our magazine, its moral success was observed by all parties." A photograph accompanying the report shows an eight-person troupe, with Soros standing behind a seated Baghy [Figure 2].

Tivadar Soros was perhaps less reluctant to appear in print and to publish his story than the editors of *Literatura Mondo* implied in their message to their readers. The very first issue of the journal, published in October 1922, carried a brief fable from India, "The Fairest Judgment" (*La plej justa juĝo*), written by Teo Melas, a pseudonym for Soros, and the November issue contained a brief review of Oswald (here called Oskar) Spengler's *Decline of the West*, signed "T.M." The inside back cover of this November 1922 issue consisted of advertisements, one of them enigmatically containing only the words "Modernaj Robinzonoj" followed by a series of question marks. This advertisement continued to appear in subsequent issues and was evidently a kind of teaser for the serialization.

Furthermore, Soros did, after all, submit the manuscript to the Manresa Floral Games – ninth in a series of literary competitions reviving a medieval Catalan tradition and launched at the World Esperanto Congress in Barcelona in 1909. So this was no shrinking literary violet.

Modernaj Robinzonoj was his only significant literary contribution to *Literatura Mondo* during the two years he remained closely associated with the magazine. While Baghy and Kalocsay were occupied with its content, Soros was primarily interested in its business side: it was his subsidy as publisher and owner that launched *Literatura Mondo* and kept it alive. Despite its paper losses, he shrewdly saw the enterprise as an investment. With hyperinflation raging, the inflow of foreign exchange from subscriptions was very helpful to him personally: he turned it into working capital which he used to exploit the extremely favorable conditions available to Hungarian investors.[2] In September

---

2 "He married my mother and, partly through that marriage and partly from profits he made on publishing an Esperanto journal, we owned a

1924 when the journal was taken over by the Hungarian Esperanto Institute, becoming institutionally rather than privately owned, his name disappeared from the masthead. An editorial message in that issue, while apologizing for the lateness of its publication, declares: "We must give special thanks to the editor-in-chief Dr. Teodoro Schwartz, who made possible and in large measure assisted the publication [of the journal] through his constant support." His name continues to appear in the list of collaborators until the end of 1924, when it drops from sight.

Literatura Mondo, its finances now as precarious as most such literary magazines, lasted only until April 1926, when it abruptly ceased publication. Revived in 1931 by Kalocsay, Baghy and others, it continued until 1938. A third period of publication began in 1947 and ended in August 1949, after the Communists consolidated their power following the elections in May of that year and most independent literary enterprises of this kind, including anything associated with Esperanto, were closed down or taken over. The magazine's demise on this occasion was permanent. Baghy died in 1967 and Kalocsay in 1976. The journal *Hungara Vivo* carried on some parts of the mission of *Literatura Mondo* in later years, and today two magazines, *Beletra Almanako* and *Literatura Foiro*, continue the tradition.

---

certain amount of real estate," says George Soros, in *Soros on Soros* (New York: John Wiley & Sons, 1995), p. 27. On the economic conditions in Hungary at the time, see Paul Ignotus, *Hungary* (New York: Praeger, 1972), who suggests (p. 153) that "government-sponsored facilities to exploit workers, employees, and consumers ... constituted an essential feature of the Counter-revolutionary Hungarian economy," and led to record profits for investors. "Measured by cash returns, the Horthy régime was a capitalists' paradise."

II

Tivadar Soros's memoir of Siberia, brief and written in a simple style, is essentially an adventure story – a story of a young man's ingenuity and endurance, composed in the style and the genre that he himself tells us he liked to read. The year is 1920. The story takes us, in the course of a few pages, from military captivity in the Russian Far East, to a journey through a ravaged and uncertain Russia, as the author seeks to return to Europe by whatever means he can devise. The journey begins with escape from captivity and with a train ride lasting more than two weeks, taking him from Khabarovsk, north of Vladivostok, to the area of deepest wilderness along the Trans-Siberian Railway, the mountain ranges north of the Amur River. From there, our author travels on foot through the mountains, finally reaching one of the rivers that drain into the Arctic Ocean. He and his companions ultimately make it to civilization by rafting down the perilous Vitim River.

Soros is quite explicit in disclaiming literary pretensions, and his narrative is unvarnished and unassuming. The very simplicity of the story perhaps contributed to its considerable popularity. "Its style gives the book a special value," declares an announcement in the August 1924 issue of *Literatura Mondo*. It describes this style as "simple, almost sketchy," but suggests that precisely because of this sketchiness it has "great expressive force and conveys a certain sympathetic spontaneity."

Soros's choice of title, "Modern Robinsons," links the book with a tradition of imitations of Defoe's *Robinson Crusoe* inspired by translations of that work into various European languages and known in those languages as *robinsonades* (the term was created by Johann Gottfried Schnabel in German in 1731, in the preface to his own imitation of Defoe, *Die Insel Felsenburg*). Such *robinsonades* are particularly numerous in German and French, and their settings include not only desert islands but even Siberian forests.³ The term works particularly well in Esperanto because the suffix *-ado* denotes a continued action, and hence *robinzonado* is an ongoing adventure of the kind experienced by Robinson Crusoe.

While Soros may have been inspired by Defoe's solitary hero, and while there are hints of a certain utopian idealism in his narrative (coupled with a cynicism about civilization and admiration for those Noble Savages the Orochons, equivalents of Crusoe's Friday), he is inconsistent in his imitation, and resemblances to Defoe's style in some of the early chapters recede and disappear in the later sections. It is, however, worth pointing out that a certain artlessness characterizes both authors and gives them much of their strength. "Defoe always wrote a prose that, formally, was rather slipshod and clumsy-seeming," Angus Ross, one of his editors, suggests.⁴

The story does not tell us the circumstances of Soros's arrival in Siberia, nor what role, or even what army, he served in. It assumes a knowledge of the background that today's reader, for the most part, does not possess (though perhaps in some sense the particulars of this background are irrelevant: this is a story about the human will to survive, regardless of such particulars). In fact he was a member of the Austro-Hungarian army. In his memoir *Maskerado ĉirkaŭ la morto* (see below), he describes how he came to enlist:

---

3 On the *robinsonade*, see Philip Babcock Gove, *The Imaginary Voyage in Prose Fiction* (London: Holland Press, 1961), pp. 122-154. The story that we today tend to regard as *Robinson Crusoe* was in reality only Part I of what ultimately became a three-part work. In the second part, Crusoe travels to, among other places, Siberia. Is it possible that our author knew this? On Crusoe in Siberia, see Arthur W. Secord, *Studies in the Narrative Method of Defoe* (Urbana: University of Illinois, 1924).

4 Angus Ross, ed. *The Life and Adventures of Robinson Crusoe* by Daniel Defoe (New York: Penguin, 1985).

> I was just twenty years old when World War I broke out. I headed for the front immediately, volunteering as a student before my studies were completed. I did so not out of patriotic enthusiasm but out of fear that the war would finish too soon. I was sure that this was the last world war: if I let it go by, I would miss a unique opportunity.[5]

He was, then, an adventurer, a young man eager to try anything and optimistic about his ability to succeed. Captured initially by the (pre-Revolutionary) Russians and sent east, he spent time in camps in a number of locations, finally ending up at Khabarovsk, in the Russian Far East. Then, in July 1918, Japan, Great Britain, France and the United States joined to send an expedition to Siberia,[6] whose purposes were somewhat obscure. In fact, each party had a goal in mind, but these goals were distinctly different. Britain and France were initially eager to open a second front against the Central Powers, in effect ignoring the Treaty of Brest-Litovsk of March 3, 1918, which, on paper at least, brought peace between the Russians and the Germans. Japan was primarily interested in bringing the Russian Far East and Siberia under Japanese political domination. As for the United States, while it expressed some support for the idea of opening a second front, it was mostly interested in containing the Japanese.[7]

With the establishment of an anti-Bolshevik government under Admiral Alexander Kolchak at Omsk in October-November 1918, the goal of the intervention changed, at least for the French and British.

---

5 Teodoro S. Ŝvarc, *Maskerado ĉirkaŭ la morto*, La Laguna, Spain: Régulo, 1965, p. 14-15. My translation.

6 See Notes for a number of books in English on this fascinating episode. Canada, Serbia, and Latvia also sent contingents to Siberia as a part of the Allied effort.

7 Here and elsewhere, I have made use of Lester H. Brune, *Chronological History of U.S. Foreign Relations 1776 to January 20, 1981* (New York and London: Garland, 1985).

Now the primary interest was to provide support for Kolchak. This new objective in effect marooned a collection of Central European soldiers in prisoner-of-war camps in the Russian Far East. These soldiers were now of no consequence to the changed nature of the hostilities: at issue now was not the overthrow of the Kaiser for whom they had fought, but the suppression of revolution in Russia. Faced with the strong military opposition of Kolchak, the Red Army retreated in the west, and its supporters in the east (of whom there were many, not least because of years of Czarist oppression in Siberia) took to waging an essentially guerilla war against Kolchak's supporters, assisted by the rugged and sparsely populated terrain in the region.

Kolchak's strong military showing in 1918 and early 1919 essentially dissipated in the face of Red resolve and a number of strategic and tactical errors. Kolchak himself, abandoning Omsk as the Red Army advanced on it in November 1919, sought to re-establish his government in Irkutsk, but was betrayed to the Reds by the Czecho-Slovak Brigade, a collection of prisoners-of-war and deserters from the Austro-Hungarian Army who formed in Kiev in 1916 and were armed by the Imperial Russian forces to fight against the Germans and Austrians. His successor, Grigorii Semenov, was little more than a warlord, whose Cossack followers, with headquarters in Chita, perpetrated numerous horrors on the population at large in the period following the collapse of Kolchak's regime.

Japan, of course, was no stranger to this part of the world, having fought a largely inconclusive war with Russia just thirteen years before. On this occasion,[8] with forces far larger than those of the other allies, Japan advanced as far as Chita and Irkutsk, but a proposed push further westwards was cut short by the armistice at the end of the year. While the armies of the other powers withdrew relatively quickly (the

---

[8] On the diplomatic processes leading to Japan's engagement in Siberia, see James W. Morley, *The Japanese Thrust into Siberia, 1918* (New York: Columbia University Press, 1957).

last to leave were the Americans in April 1920),[9] Japanese troops remained on the mainland until they finally agreed to leave in October 1922 in response to American diplomatic pressure. They continued their occupation of the island of Sakhalin, immediately to the north of Japan, until 1925. It should perhaps be added that American efforts in Siberia were relatively benign, aimed, as much as anything, at humanitarian assistance and at preventing the other major powers from meddling. General Graves, the American commander, also worked hard to limit Cossack atrocities. It is perhaps not surprising that the British and Japanese tended to see him as pro-Communist.

Soros and his companions, then, were prisoners of war representing an imperial Austrian government no longer in existence which had in recent years enjoyed very little support in Hungary and had become fully subservient to Germany. Under such circumstances, it was hard to develop a sense of meaningful loyalties and difficult to avoid a kind of all-encompassing cynicism.

The marginal nature of this population of Austro-Hungarians cannot be emphasized too strongly: they were essentially pawns in the hands of whomever chose to make use of them. Soros was an officer in an army that no longer existed. Many Austrians and Hungarians, most of them imprisoned further to the west, were, as of 1919, regaining their freedom, and many of them were recruited into the White Army. Although others entered the Red Army, Hungarian nationality was hardly a sign of trustworthiness to the Reds, and Hungarians who ended up in Red hands could not expect any special sympathy. At the same time, they were on the losing side in the First World War, and so they were no friends of the Americans, British or Japanese either. Of course, with the withdrawal of the Americans, British and French,

---

9 All Americans were transported by train from the Lake Baikal region to Vladivostok between January 15 and January 25, 1920. They began their evacuation on February 15, with further contingents embarking on March 10, 20, and 31, and the final group leaving on April 1.

the prisoners were largely left to the tender mercies of the Russian population, among them the bloodthirsty and ruthless anti-Bolshevik Cossacks under the local control of Ataman Kalmykov, whose sadistic cruelties offended even his own men. If we add to all of this the fact that the Whites were particularly anti-Semitic and Soros was a Jew, he was on no one's list as a friend – and he was well aware of that fact.

His son Paul recalls his mentioning that the Reds overran another prisoner of war camp in the same general area as the one at Khabarovsk. They immediately executed the leadership among the prisoners. Tivadar Soros was a prisoners' representative – a leader in the camp at Khabarovsk. He told Paul that this was one of the main reasons why he chose to break out when he did. The Cossacks would probably have been no friendlier than the Reds, given the opportunity.

It is remarkable that so little of this political and military detail finds a place in Soros's narrative. Indeed, the narrative seems almost suspended in political space. Perhaps this is what his reviewer meant by referring to the story as "simple, almost sketchy." His intention, of course, was to tell an adventure story, and to focus on incident rather than on historical background. He may also have felt, writing just a year or two after his return, that the author of a narrative in a literary journal going all over the world, and particularly the countries of Europe, including the Soviet Union, needed to be particularly careful not to offend any of that journal's readers. This may be the reason why he did not continue the narrative further than he did: the story ends with its hero still thousands of miles from home, in an environment politically as well as physically hostile. While there is little overt criticism of the new order in Russia, it is clear that the Bolshevik view of the world was not one with which Tivadar Soros had a great deal of sympathy, though his internationalist and humanitarian views hardly put him in sympathy with the other side, such as it was, either.

In Siberia, protecting himself against his fellow human beings was only part of Tivadar Soros's challenge. He also faced a desperately hostile physical environment. Siberia was still largely undeveloped. The port of Vladivostok, in the Russian Far East, was founded in 1860, but it was not until the early 1900s that it was linked by rail to the rest of Russia – by way of Manchuria and its capital Harbin. The final route of the Trans-Siberian Railway, including the Amur line which skirted northern Manchuria, did not open to traffic until 1916. Up until then, there were two ways of reaching Vladivostok – either through Manchuria or by ship from the end of the railroad line, down the Amur River, to Khabarovsk, where the Ussuri line went south to Vladivostok. The interior, or Siberia proper (the Russians distinguish between the Far East – the region around Vladivostok and Khabarovsk – and Siberia) was largely without roads, and its population was limited to various nomadic tribes and to mining settlements along the major rivers. It was also a place of vast distances: thousands of miles of empty territory separated its settlements from the west.

The custom of using Siberia as a dumping-ground for the unwanted – criminals, ethnic undesirables, political prisoners – has a long history, extending back to the reign of Peter the Great. In effect the prisoner-of-war camps were a continuation of this tradition. Making his way through the mountainous territory north of the Amur – some of the most inhospitable country in all of Russia – was a challenge indeed to Tivadar Soros. According to Paul Soros, for example, the story in Chapter 4, of Dolfi and Sepi and their practice of cannibalism, was more than a story out of the past, associated with two people essentially unconnected with Tivadar: later Tivadar told his son that there was serious talk of cannibalism as the adventurers slogged their way towards the Vitim River, and on at least one occasion it might well have occurred but for Tivadar's intervention.

It is not easy to determine the precise route that Soros and his party followed through the wilderness, but the notes to the text provide what seems a plausible reconstruction, and several questions could no doubt be solved by a good Russian-speaking historian with access to the appropriate sources. In essence, the party headed north from Ksenievka as far as the Olekma River, and then took a curving route to the west to reach the Vitim River. Even today, the territory through which they trekked is without permanent settlements: whole sections of the maps prepared by Soviet cartographers show no signs of human habitation at all, beyond tracks through the forest used by loggers, hunters, or prospectors. Moving through this territory without proper maps, without adequate equipment, and largely without experience must have been a trial indeed, and it is truly remarkable that the journey was completed at all, and apparently without loss of life.

The story ends with the arrival of the party on the lower reaches of the Vitim. Just how Soros made his way to Moscow we do not know, nor do his family members have much knowledge of it. Arriving in Moscow, he apparently had fairly active contact with Esperanto speakers, according to his son Paul, and this may have been the point at which he learned the language and began to participate in the Esperanto movement. But in Moscow he was still not free to return to Hungary, or at least not without further bold and imaginative efforts, as he explains in *Maskerado*:

> My first successful play-acting as an adult took place under rather different circumstances when I was 27 or 28 years old. In the summer of 1919 the Communist regime of Béla Kun collapsed in Hungary. The four months of his "Red Terror" were followed by Horthy's "White Terror." At the time I was in a Russian prisoner of war camp. The Russians refused to allow the return of Hungarian officers who were prisoners of war. Their plan was to keep them as hostages in order to curb the excesses of the Hungarian authorities against their communist captives. Austrians were leaving at a rate of five hundred a week. I watched them sadly. Seven years of war and prison camp made me very anxious to get back home. By chance, I got hold of a Baedecker guide for the Austrian city of Linz. The book was full of maps

and pictures. I studied it with care and then presented myself to the repatriation committee as an Austrian, born in Linz. It worked: I answered all their questions correctly and they scheduled me to leave, as an Austrian officer, on August 14, 1921.[10]

Such ingenuity, and such an instinct for survival, characterized so much of what Tivadar Soros did in his life. He was to employ these qualities again in Budapest in World War II, where Jewish survival depended upon outwitting the authorities and using all the ingenuity at one's disposal.

III

Following the publication of his story and the completion of his stewardship of *Literatura Mondo*, Tivadar Soros became less visible on the Hungarian Esperanto scene, though he seems to have remained a loyal and somewhat active member of the Esperanto movement throughout the 1930s. The coming of World War II and, finally, the German occupation of Hungary, brought him once again, as we have seen, face to face with mortal danger. His native ingenuity once again stood him in good stead, when he and his wife and two sons all navigated their way through the war under his guidance, and against the odds. Just how much against the odds is clear from the statistics:

> By the end of the war some two-thirds of Hungary's Jewish population (practicing and converted), including some 40 per cent of those in Budapest, were exterminated. On the whole territory which during the war was supposed to be run by Hungarians, about 600,000 Jews lost their lives.[11]

The story of how Tivadar and his family survived those desperate years was later told in Esperanto in his *Maskerado ĉirkaŭ la morto* (1965, trans-

---

10 *Maskerado*, p. 46.
11 Paul Ignotus, *Hungary*, p. 191.

lated as *Maskerado: Dancing Around Death in Nazi Hungary*[12]), a more extensive memoir than *Modernaj Robinzonoj*, but characterized again by a matter-of-fact style and an enduring sense of optimism. It was one of the earliest of what subsequently became an established genre – the Central European Jewish survival narrative. *Maskerado*, fittingly, was published by Juan Régulo, another survivor, veteran of the losing side in the Spanish civil war, who in the late 1940s founded the publishing house Stafeto, the most important publisher of Esperanto literature in the post-war years just as Literatura Mondo occupied that role in the 1920s and 1930s. Régulo provided a preface.

Tivadar's son George left Hungary for England by way of Bern, where, in 1947, the first post-war World Esperanto Congress took place. Tivadar, Paul, and George all signed up to attend, according to the congress handbook, though Paul in fact did not go.[13] Tivadar and George got themselves included in the delegation from Hungary permitted to travel to Bern. George stayed on in Switzerland until his British visa came through and he went on to an Esperanto youth conference in Ipswich. Acquiring a student visa in Britain through his Esperanto contacts, George ended up at the London School of Economics and ultimately moved to the United States. Paul left Hungary definitively a couple of years later as a member of the Hungarian Olympic ski team, defecting in Austria and ultimately reaching the United States, where he later established a highly successful engineering business. Tivadar and Elizabeth made the same journey in 1956, moving to New York by way of Vienna. Tivadar was an active member of the New York Esperanto Society and attended the World Esperanto Congresses in Tokyo in 1965 and Budapest in 1966.

---

12 Edinburgh: Canongate, 2000. Published in the United States as *Masquerade: Dancing Around Death in Nazi-Occupied Hungary* (New York: Arcade Publishing, 2001).

13 George Soros gives a brief account of this episode in *Soros on Soros*, p. 31.

Tivadar Soros has been characterized as a survivor, and certainly both of his books testify to such an instinct, and also to his sharply utilitarian approach to the affairs of the world. Less obvious, but equally powerful in these two books, is a strong sense of idealism, a love of family, and an extraordinary generosity. He was a huge influence on his two sons, as both have attested. But his qualities were recognized also by those outside his family who came into contact with him. A week or so after his death at his home on Riverside Drive on February 22, 1968, a memorial meeting took place at the Ethical Church on Central Park West. Mark Starr, a longtime friend and associate in the New York Esperanto Society, and a prominent labor leader, paid tribute to his profound influence on the Esperanto movement and its literature. But he went on to talk also about his personal qualities, about how he "supported the ordinary man in freedom and justice against all dictators" and how his memoirs of World War II displayed "his courage to help others when the Nazi murderers came." "Instead of egotism, nationalism and chauvinism," said Starr, "he thought of Universal Man." "Theodore Schwartz," added Starr, using the name by which Soros was known in the Esperanto movement, "affirmed life through his essential goodness and gave us faith in humankind. Let us not forget his example."

H.T.

Notes on the Translation

U.S. style has been used throughout (e.g. American railroad terminology rather than British, American spelling). Tivadar Soros's connections were with the United States rather than Britain, and accordingly this seems the more natural translating strategy.

All references to Russian weights and measures (versts, poods) have been converted silently to their British and American equivalents.

Wherever possible, I have checked current transliterations of Russian place names and used these modern forms.

Tivadar Soros was some 28 years old when, shortly after his return from military captivity in Siberia, he and several of his Esperanto-speaking friends launched the literary journal *Literatura Mondo* and the publishing operation of the same name. The first issue of the journal bore the date October 1922.

POST LA XV-A

Pri la belaj horoj kaj gravaj decidoj de la kongreso raportos aliaj presorganoj, ni, por eviti eĉ ŝajnon de konkuro, volas nin teni severe fakaj kaj ne forvagi el la literaturaj kampoj al fremdaj al ni teritorioj.

Sole la ĉiam kortuŝa kaj neforgeseble profunda impreso de la malferma himnokantado, kunforĝanta la animojn en kvazaŭ ekstazan unuecon, estu ĉi tie menciata. Kaj la malferma parolado de sdo Privat, por kio kaj por kiu jam estas banala ĉiu epiteto. Espereble ĝi aperos komplete en la „Esperanto", ĉiu povos ĝin legi por plezuro kaj por ĉerpo de entuziasmo. Bedaŭrinde, ke la indiferentaj plumbliteroj ne povas prezenti ankaŭ la ĉarmon de lia vivanta parolo.

Pri la impresa prezentado de Natan la Saĝulo ni raportas aliloke.

Rilate al la teatraj prezentadoj de L. M. ni povas, sen fanfarono, raporti pri vera sukceso. Estis malfacilaĵoj grandaj kaj kompreneblaj, la L. K. K., inter sia multa peno kaj zorgo povis doni al ni nur iom duonpatrinan zorgemon, sur la scenejon

„Ni venis ja, laŭveste, Malriĉe, kaj modeste"
kaj la fatala akustiko de la Ĉambrego glutis kaj glutis. Tamen, kvankam, pro diversaj kaŭzoj ĺa materiala flanko de nia entrepreno ne povis esti tiel prospera, ke ni povus per ĝi iom plifortikigi la financan bazon de nia revuo, — la morala sukceso estis konstatata de ĉiuj plej diversaj flankoj.

Ĉi tiun sukceson ni ne atribuas al ni mem, nek al la interna valoro de nia programo. La aplaŭdojn gajnis por ni la Lingvo, kiu deskuinte la katenojn de la diletantismo, devis montri tiujn mirindajn vivfortojn, kiujn sin kaŝas en ĝi. Iom malica rideto de milda ironio; korŝiraj sonoj de patrina doloro; subtila sentimentaleco de moderna kanzono; naiva sed forta voĉo de l' kamparo; artifika trosttremigo de l' ruzefarita teruro, melankoliaj rebriloj de l' romantika revemo; ekstaza patoso de l' vundita animo; pikanta ĉarmo de petola fabelo; spi itaj transkapiĝoj de l' plej kurioza ŝerco, jen la plej diversaj kolornuancoj, en kiuj nia Diamanto povis briligi siajn facetojn. Ĉi tiu malriĉa kaj modesta prezentado sukcesis eble montri, ke — uzante la vortojn de la Prologo

En la literaturo la lingvo vivas, spiras, El ĝi la freŝon, riĉon, potencon ĝi akiras. Ne nur ornam' ĝi estas, ĝi estas garantio De nepereigebla vivanta energio. Ĝi estas flora arb' kaj ne estas ĝia floro La flor' artefarita, sen vivo, sen odoro, Kiun kun ruz' naiva, harfende kaj komplike La ĉambrofilologoj fabrikas artifike. Kaj estu ĝi fruktarbo, por kies dolĉa bero Amase venos ĉiuj popoloj de la Tero, Ke, kiel la abeloj, ĝin svarme ĉirkaŭzumu, Avide ĝin sopiru, soife ĝui gustumu.

Sed, — diras plu la Prologo :

Nia arbo estas ankoraŭ arb' sovaĝa . . . Ĉu pro malfort' de gusto, ĉu pro gustetoj flankaj La dolĉaj frukt-aromoj kelkfoje estas mankaj. Do ni ĝin devas grefti, nobligi kun fervoro. Hej, bonaj ĝardenistoj, bonvenon por laboro! Jam por ĉi tiu arbo la grundon ni forbaris, Ĝardenon sukoplenan, agrablan ni preparis.

LA TEATRA TRUPETO DE L. M.

Hevesi, Schwartz, C. Pechan,
Sárosay, A. Pechan, Baghy, Noiret, Kalocsay

Jen estas nia programo. Nia unua jaro baldaŭ finiĝos. En la unua numero ni parolis pri niaj revoj — ili grandparte restis revoj. Ĉu ili restu revoj por ĉiam ? Tio dependas de vi, kara popolo Esperanta. Abonu kaj abonigu nian revuon. Kaj — renovigu vian abonon senprokraste, se ĝi, kiel ĉe multaj, finiĝos jam je la septembra numero. La malproksimoj estas grandaj kaj ni volus vidi klare, ĉu nia revuo povas jam stari sur propraj piedoj aŭ ni eble povas ĝin eĉ pliampleksigi. Vere la kadroj estas tro malvastaj, kaj ni havas tre multajn, bonajn, longajn manuskriptojn, kies sendintojn ni devas peti pri pacienco. Ni ekiris por atako kontraŭ la manko de loko kaj ĝi nun triumfos ankaŭ ĉe ni — se vi ne helpas, per abono kaj abonigo, pligrandigi la paĝnombron de la revuo.

Pardonu pro la subita proza tono, eble ni povos pravigi nin, citante denove el la Prologo:

Per via helpo certe prosperos nia verko . . . Sed por la arbo estas necesa — ankaŭ sterko. Kaj evidente estas ĉi tiu sterk' — la mono. Jen, kial sonas, kara publiko la admono Kaj peto por subteno: por lego kaj abono.

Ĝis revido — en la sekvonta kongreso, kie ni volus al vi prezenti jon surprizan. Ĝis tiam — sukcesan propagandon.

Samideane : LA REDAKTA KOMITATO.

The team of Soros, Kalocsay and Baghy was extraordinary by any measure. When, for the World Esperanto Congress in Nuremberg in 1923, they teamed up to present a cabaret, their performance was, according to fellow-Espe-

(2a)

rantist and historian Edmond Privat, "a veritable feast of good taste and linguistic brilliance." The August 1923 issue of *Literatura Mondo* reports on their triumphs. A photograph accompanying the report shows an eight-person troupe, with Soros (back row, middle) standing behind a seated Baghy. Kalocsay is on the right.

On the opposite side, you see the entire page of *Literatura Mondo*; its center photograph has been enlarged, digitally enhanced, and reproduced above.

ANONCOJ:
GRANDAJ LAŬ INTERKONSENTO!
MALGRANDAJ:
PO DU ENPRESOJ LA PREZO DE UNU NUMERO!
PAGO NEPRE ANTAŬE!

Nia sola semajna gazeto estas la
ESPERANTO TRIUMFONTA
Internacia! Semajna! Neŭtrala!
Nepre abonu ĝin!
Abonejoj en ĉiuj landoj
Administracio:
Horrem bei Köln, Germ.

INTERNACIA FOIRO EN PRAHA
(Ĉeĥoslovakujo)
Informojn donas: PRAŽSKÉ VZORKOVÉ VELETRHY Staroměststká radnice PRAHA I
Esperantu korespondata!

Nenia resaniĝo — nenia pago!
ASTMULOJ!
PLI OL 20000 suferintoj pro astmo kronika, bronka, nerva, estas tute aŭ parte resanigitaj pere de
VIVAMOL
(antaŭe Vixol).

Tiu elpensaĵo de nia samideano E. Ĉefeĉ estas kuracilo plej taŭga por ĉiuj astmuloj. Ĝi enhavas nenian drogon danĝeran.

Senpaga trisemajna provado!

ONI BEZONAS AGENTOJN.

Petu broŝuron de
VIVAMOL, Ltd. III. Gt.
PORTLAND St., LONDON W. I.

La evoluon de la grafikaj industrioj servas la interesa
MAGYAR GRAFIKA
(HUNGARA GRAFIKO)
BUDAPEST VI, ARADI-UTCA 8
Ĉiuj, kiujn interesas la grafiko de l' arto, mendu ĝin! Unu numero kostas hungaran K· 250.—

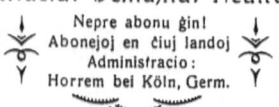**ODERNAJ ROBINZONOJ!**
? ? ? ? ? ? ? ? ? ? ? ?

Könyves Kálmán
r.-t.
Fama eldonejo de reproduktaĵoj por artaj bildoj! Desegnaĵoj, pentraĵoj de mondfamaj artistoj! Rekomendas siajn eldonaĵojn Petu ilustritan prezaron!

Budapest VI, Nagymező-utca 37-39

ESPERANTO SERVICE CORPORATION „ESKO"
500 FIFTH AVENUE NEW-YORK CITY
Telegrafa adreso: ESPERANTO NEW-YORK
Aĉeto, eksporto, importo kaj maklerado de ĉiuspecaj komercaĵoj
Katalogoj, prezaroj kaj specimenoj estas danke ricevataj

ORIENTO!
Havigu al vi tuj la intereseplenajn literatur-historiajn verkojn, kun trikoloraj etnografiaj kartoj, en plej konciza Esperanto, laŭditaj de ĉiuj: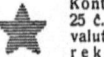
LA BULGARA LANDO KAJ POPOLO LA NAJBAROJ DE RUSLANDO
Kontraŭ 1 dol., 5 sv. fr., 10 fr. fr., 25 ĉ. kr., 500 g. mk. (laŭ la monvaluto de l' mendinto) sendas rekomendite la aŭtoro:
IVAN H. KRESTANOFF
Dresden--A., Wintergartenstrasse 9. German

The inside back cover of the November 1922 *Literatura Mondo* consisted of advertisements, one of them enigmatically containing only the words "Modernaj Robinzonoj" followed by a series of question marks. This advertisement continued to appear in subsequent issues and was evidently a kind of teaser for the serialization.

Illustrations   *Literatura Mondo*

Seven monthly installments of *Modernaj Robinzonoj* appeared in the magazine, the last published in the December 1923 issue. In February 1924 the magazine already carried an advertisement announcing the publication of the complete text.

Modernaj Robinzonoj, when it finally appeared early in 1924, actually bore two dates and two publishers. The cover announced that it was a publication of Literatura Mondo and carried the date 1924.

Illustrations   *Literatura Mondo*

DRO. TEODORO SCHWARTZ

MODERNAJ ROBINZONOJ

EN LA SIBERIA PRAARBARO

PREMIITA
DUM LA IX. INT. FLORAJ LUDOJ
EN MANRESA

1 9 2 3
GLOBUS PRESARTINSTITUTO AKCIA SOCIETO
BUDAPEST

The title page, on the other hand, gave "Globus Presartinstituto Akcia Societo" as the publisher and the date 1923. Globus Institute of Printing Arts was the printer of the magazine *Literatura Mondo* and the volumes published under the Literatura Mondo name, so the title page may simply represent confusion of printer and publisher or may indicate that originally Soros contracted with Globus for a kind of private printing, bringing the little book under the umbrella of Literatura Mondo shortly before it was actually published.

Crusoes in Siberia

Introduction

Once upon a time, many years ago, when I was still a child, my dearest mother asked me, with that sweetness only a loving mother knows how to express, "Well, my little lad, what do you want to be when you grow up?"

And I replied with all the pride of a seven- or eight-year-old, "An explorer — a discoverer."

I remember how my mother laughed, stroking my dark hair affectionately with her gentle hands. "You poor little innocent!" she cried. "By the time you grow up, there will be nothing left to explore or discover."

My childish heart grew heavy. I would gladly have grown up right there and then, to stay ahead of the rest of the world! I envied such people as Robinson Crusoe, Stanley, Columbus, and those others who were lucky enough to be born and flourish before me.

Many years have passed since then — long years of suffering. But as I begin the story of my adventures in the virgin forest of Siberia I am reminded again of that childhood dream.

Worse luck, my dream came true. Fate, capricious as always, drove me to the farthest east and left me to wander through thousands of miles of Siberian forest, in the mysterious and dangerous taiga.

In providing this brief account of what occurred, I have no intention of writing an enduring work of literature. Lacking such power of the pen, I will merely offer a true account of my experiences and my reactions to them. My aim is simple: to provide a remembrance of human pain and suffering experienced in this twentieth century, the so-called "century of humanity."

Read these words and never dream of becoming – Robinson Crusoe!

CHAPTER I
Captivity

In which our kind reader is informed of the pleasures of prisoners of war, of the humane conduct of warring parties and of something that permits the continuation of this story.

Where the Manchurian border touches eastern Siberia, at the confluence of two mighty rivers, the Ussuri and the Amur, lies the city of Khabarovsk.[1] In the neighborhood of that bustling and effervescent city lay a graveyard for living beings – a camp for prisoners of war. Its heavy, ungainly barracks kept the lives of over two thousand prisoners in perpetual shackles, and the red bricks of its walls seemed to reflect the bloodthirstiness of their builders. These unyielding bricks stared blankly out at barbed-wire fences. Behind these fences lived a miserable collection of Germans, Turks, Hungarians, forced into war by the vagaries of the twentieth century. Living in these crypts for three or four years, in some cases even six or seven, and mourning the stolen springtime of their lives, the inhabitants turned into old men – people who had enjoyed none of the pleasures of this paradise called earth.

At the time, Siberia was the scene of major political upheavals. In 1918, the Allies decided on military intervention to pacify (for their own profit) the various political factions. In Vladivostok, some 300 miles from Khabarovsk, their ships disgorged armies of soldiers of various colors and nations. Frenchmen, Englishmen, Canadians, Americans, Italians, Chinese and Japanese joined one another to defend the highest principles of humanity...[2]

Our prison camp was in the American and Japanese spheres of interest, and the two nations took it in turns to "capture" its inhabitants so that they could announce their great achievements to the world.[3]

In this way, I had the honor of being made a prisoner of war not once but three times over. First the Russians, then the Americans, and finally the Japanese served as my hosts, without prior invitation and with heartwarming generosity. This seemingly unimportant change in management in fact had significant financial consequences. The ruble lost value daily, and we, as officers, received 25 dollars, and later 50 yen, instead of 50 rubles – a 500-fold increase. Accordingly, many thousands of prisoners living in Siberia were eager to be captured by the American army. On one occasion, after hearing a deputation of supplicants, who described in sincere and heart-rending words the situation of the prisoners of war in Petropavlovsk, two thousand of whom had died in two months from typhoid fever brought on from lack of food, the head of the American Red Cross replied that "America has only tears to relieve the suffering, not money" – and gave them a few rosaries and prayer books.

Our financial situation did indeed improve, and we became known as "the POW millionaires." But really we were only "millionaires of misery" and no one in a similar situation could truly envy us. The majority of our fellow-prisoners, deprived of any news of their homes and families, looked forward only to a black and melancholy future. The constant uncertainty, a social life completely without women, the crowded conditions (60 or 70 people per room), the poisonous stench of stale air and disease-ridden breath, not only broke our physical health but also destroyed our mental equilibrium. The sense of enslavement brought despair, and the imaginative powers of inflamed minds led to madness. Every day served to increase the numbers of those whose mental state could no longer bear the burden of the life of a "millionaire," with all the cares it brought with it.

How we envied the very people outside the camp who envied us! It is true that they led lives of grinding poverty, but at least they could circulate freely and occasionally forget their miseries. Our constant complaint was always the same: "What can we do? What can we do?" There seemed to be no answer.

Morov, head of the American regiment, promised early repatriation, but the promise remained nothing more than a promise.[4] His Excellency General Janin, of the French army,[5] even sent a handwritten letter promising his help, but the ships he promised had yet to appear on the blue horizon, and in fact he had no ships to offer. But sympathy is a pretty virtue and costs nothing. He even pledged immediate assistance if we were prepared to march west through the Urals, rifles in hand, to break through the Bolshevik front, of whose advance there were ever more threatening rumors (this was the time of the Russian General Kolchak's retreat from Omsk.)[6] Every month came a new promise and we were regaled every month with some further deception. Little by little, an overwhelming pessimism spread its wings over us, and their melancholy shadow shut out even the feeblest spark of hope. Our teeth were gritted in silence, only occasionally uttering the customary complaints –

"I can't go on any longer."

"I haven't had a letter for five years."

"My little daughter won't recognize me."

"I was eighteen when I was drafted into the army, and now I'm 24. Who will give me my youth back? What can I do? Where can I go?"

Where? More or less anywhere to get away from this treadmill, this grindstone of men's souls. To escape and fly to open air, to a distant country, to the loving embrace of parents or fiancée.... It was such feelings as this that gave birth to our first thoughts of breaking out....

Eastwards, towards Vladivostok, security was very tight, and more than one escaped prisoner had been brought back from as far away as

Canada. To the west, General Kolchak's military front, while it was fraught with a thousand dangers, might, with a little luck, present possibilities....

"Next spring!" We repeated this phrase constantly, and with it our peace of mind and our courage grew. The Siberian winter lasts from October to June. He who hesitates or fails to take advantage of the more favorable weather, loses everything – everything. Escape! That was our only salvation!

The study of Russian assumed epidemic proportions in the camp, and everyone began learning a trade. It did not take me long to realize that a doctoral diploma was not worth much if you had to earn your daily bread in a foreign country, and so, in the year 1919, I became the hard-working apprentice of a machinist and locksmith, feeling that this trade would help me prosper on my long journey. Every day I had to push myself to go to work: the unaccustomed activity wore me out. But such exhaustion was in its way the happiest benefit of seven or eight hours of work: it lulled me into a dreamless sleep.

Political circumstances, which had such an impact on the otherwise tranquil and indifferent life of the camp, suddenly shifted radically. Given such realities, it made no sense to claim a lack of interest in politics, as some of our people did, or to say that politics had nothing to do with us, because outside political events in fact turned everything upside down in those crypts with their barbed-wire fences – and the upheaval finally planted seeds of hope in our minds.

The Siberian military campaign had died a miserable death as public lack of sympathy grew among the great powers. General Kolchak's government, aware of the complete failure of its efforts, chose to withdraw and leave the field to a new regime. The first forces to leave Siberia were the Italians, French, Chinese, and English. The Russian press, its allegiance bought with Japanese money, launched a propaganda attack against the American troops who remained behind, sarcastically suggesting that "America seems to think that Siberia is a trough from which every ox can drink." Finally America also came to its senses and recalled its soldiers.[7]

The Japanese army alone stayed on in Siberia, and the Red Army advanced on it with giant steps. On February 10, 1920, they reached Irkutsk, the gateway to Mongolia, and took the city.[8] Helpless to affect the outcome, but with a deep sense of uneasiness, we prisoners waited haplessly for these two colossal forces to collide. We were consumed with impatience, mixed understandably with fear – not because we cared about the future of Siberia or the military fortunes of one or the other army, but because our own futures were at stake.

Battlefield reports and assorted gossip spread among us by over-excited optimists or pessimists, made the great theatrical spectacle on which our lives depended seem almost cinematic in its extremes. Word reached us, for example, that in Soviet Russia there were no prisoners of war left because the government had sent them all home. How many tears, how much suffering resulted from this false information! How many human lives were later sacrificed because of this well-intentioned effort to make us feel better! But we believed what we heard – and decided to act.

We had had enough! Here we were, still waiting hopelessly on the Chinese border two years after the armistice had been signed and sealed. The governments had done nothing for us, and so we had to remedy our unhappy condition by taking matters into our own hands.

The eyes of some of our fellow-prisoners took on a certain furtive brightness, and every day more and more people whispered the same question: "You too?" We all understood what they were referring to: escape, soon. The reply was as simple as the question, but delivered with a small, hopeful smile: "Me too!"

Without warning, the Japanese high command decided to abandon the western part of Khabarovsk, the Amur District, where our camp was, and the commander-in-chief bade farewell, desiring good fortune to the long-suffering Russian people. Finally! Now was the time to act!

Outside, a forty-degree frost gripped the earth, but inside, in our prison-camp crypts, we waited, hopefully and impatiently, for the final thaw. Freedom floated enticingly over the pale blue snow like the odor of distant violets!

CHAPTER II
Escape

In which the reader discovers that it is not enough simply to decide to escape.

To the prisoners, weary and despondent, the decision to escape was like first rain after a long drought. Escape was a way of asserting our independence, our manhood, our will.

We could not escape before the beginning of March because, however much we might long for fresh air and freedom, none of us felt like leaving our February officer's salary (50 yen, or today some two million Austrian crowns) sitting in the Japanese state treasury.

"Who knows?" thought the future fugitives, "We're bound to need some cash in our pockets!"

On the first of March we could already discern, as we looked out of the windows of the camp, a few dark tracks on the snowy covering of the Amur River – the first escapees. I should add that our escape was not exactly carried out with skillful precision of the kind described in *The Count of Monte Cristo*,[9] and people planned to take with them only the most essential objects.

On the morning of March 3, 1920, I collected in a backpack everything I felt necessary or usable, and put my small capital (110 yen) into a purse under my shirt. Noting the addresses of a few comrades so that I could bring word to their families upon my arrival, I put my decision to escape into effect.

"Be sure to write! In a few days, I'll follow you." Such were the words of a chorus of friends as two comrades and I, with the help of forged passes, departed our hated camp. Of course there were some who organized more romantic escape routes, such as crawling under the barbed-wire fence or hiding themselves in trash carts.

Even beyond the fence we were not entirely out of danger. There were Japanese detachments on guard, patrolling in all directions. Our false passes were valid only at a distance of one verst, some two-thirds of a mile, from the camp. Accordingly we were careful to avoid reunions with our good friends the Japanese.

A river[10] a couple of miles wide separated us from Khabarovsk. We had often longingly contemplated the city from the windows of our barracks. Just reaching the river bank made us breathe more freely, but we were also very conscious of the strong, angry wind that pelted our eyes, ears and necks with ice crystals and obscured our tracks under a blanket of whiteness.

Our route took us into the wind. The icy cold penetrated to our very bones, and we were forced to stop from time to time to massage those parts of our heads exposed to the elements. Yet we moved with such great determination through the waist-high snow that our shirts grew damp with sweat. Our feet pumped mechanically, but little by little our movements grew tired. In the middle of the river we rested. How good it felt to cover ourselves in the snow and breathe the sharp air through our open mouths! Only those who have been soldiers or have known forced marches can understand the feeling. But, despite our every effort, the course that we followed, normally a journey of two hours, took six hours to complete because of the wind.

Arriving in the city of Khabarovsk, we found some 250 or 300 prisoners of war already there. Every bar, café, bistro was already full of them. The Russians were very polite to us, calling us "citizen" and greeting with benevolent smiles our more or less enthusiastic admiration of every pretty girl or shop window. Needless to say, we were full of lively good humor, as though we had suddenly rediscovered our youth. Everything seemed in order for the execution of our plan. Until recently the inhabitants of the city and the advancing Japanese had been in a state of undeclared guerrilla war, and so the railroad line was constantly sabotaged; but following the Japanese cessation of hostilities the partisans[11] re-emerged from the forest and, working side by side with their former enemies, repaired the lines to facilitate the anticipated evacuation of the Japanese army.

"Have you heard? The first train for Russia leaves tomorrow," declared an engineer friend whom I ran into on Bolshoi Street.

"We'll hitch a ride," I replied with a self-confident smile. "If worst comes to worst, we'll glue ourselves to the wheels."

And so, first thing in the morning, we stood in line at the ticket window and, after a great deal of pushing and shoving, managed to obtain tickets, though we had resolved to travel without them if need be. The train, consisting of forty cattle cars, carried some 2000 sick and wounded. Prisoners of war were categorized among the sick. I squeezed myself in with fifty other travelers. Sardines in a can were not more tightly wedged than we were, yet we welcomed the press of people because the warmth of our bodies made up for the lack of heat.

No one knew the train's final destination. Some said that we would go non-stop to Moscow; others had doubts and predicted no more than a few hundred miles. Overall, this was a difference of opinion of some four or five thousand miles. We awaited the train's departure for several hours, our teeth chattering in the cold. We waited and waited.... But the train stayed rooted to the spot. Suddenly an officer appeared in front of the train, flushed with agitation at the news he was about to report.

"Have you heard? The Japanese have killed three prisoners of war right outside the hospital. They were trying to escape. The people on sentry duty noticed them and Captain Uheda ordered them shot dead."

Cries of protest at such terrible brutality erupted from the train.

"Who did they shoot?" asked the prisoners.

"Piros, Gerber; I forget the name of the third."

These three young men's tragic end, dead before they had a chance to live, upset us all. But our emotions were so numbed that we soon forgot all about it, except perhaps to thank our lucky stars that it had not happened to us.

Finally, the train began to move. Optimistic mathematicians calculated the average daily speed needed to reach Europe in three weeks. The only problem was that none of the railway officials could actually tell us where we were finally headed.

The locomotive crawled forward, slowly pulling the train behind it. It took six days to reach Blagoveschensk.[12] Here, one of the railway officials with whom I discussed our unhappy condition argued strongly against my continuing the journey.

"You're best off if you stay here," he said. "You'll find work in the city. Living is cheap, and you'll manage. Further along, life is at a standstill and everyone's starving, because the Japanese are still occupying the Zabaykal area.[13] For your own good, stay here until the situation improves."

For a few of us the well-intentioned warning worked, but most decided to continue the journey.

For a further ten days we jolted slowly onwards, and the distance covered reached a bare 500 miles. Knocked-out bridges along the way had to be replaced with improvised structures of logs and railroad ties.

All this while we had no access to newspapers, though at the time any news might have made a big difference to our plans.

Chapter II — Escape

Finally, in the middle of the night, the train stopped. Word quickly came to us that a military front lay ahead and we could go no further.[14] We wandered despondently along the track, cursing the entire adventure. What could we do now? Push on? Go back? And how could there be fighting up ahead, given the Japanese peace declaration?

In our aimless wandering up and down, we noticed that two railroad cars were being attached to the engine.

With my broken Russian, I went over to find out what was going on.

"*Kuda?* Where are you going?"

"To Ksenievskaya."

"There's a partisan headquarters there and they have work for us," one of the Russians explained.

"Could you take me too?"

"Citizens are not allowed to travel with railroad workers. Are you a worker?"

I returned to my fellow-prisoners with the news. At once eleven of them announced that they wanted to be railroad workers. That same night we left the others behind.

Ksenievskaya.[15] The last station. A small village, where nature provided nothing – except gold. Once when I asked someone, referring to the two warring parties, whether the locals supported the Reds or the Whites, "The Yellows," was the reply. Gold was their only love.

We started work. The burden of our daily tasks was lightened by the hope that we could soon continue our journey. But the hope was vain: days stretched into weeks and weeks into months. More and more prisoners of war appeared in the area. We discussed our situation many times, and hatched all kinds of fantastic plans to improve it – but in vain. We knew only one thing – that once June and July were gone, nothing but the terrible Siberian winter, which we knew and feared, lay ahead.

Three months had passed from the day of our departure from the camp, and all that we had to show for our adventurous decision was that out here, where it snows on May 25 and a coat of whiteness feet thick covers everything, we could, at the end of a day of work punishing to body and soul, dine on salted fish.[16]

We had to make a decision. And so on May 29 we convened the prisoners of war from the various local stations for a final discussion of our future.

CHAPTER III
Consultation

In this chapter the reader learns that it is no simple matter to travel through virgin forest.

May 29 was, then, the day of decision. As if to mark the occasion, and in preparation for new adventures, nature herself suddenly changed her clothes. Everything turned green, brilliantly green. In Siberia the transition from winter to summer occurs quickly, as if the trees, anticipating their short season of enjoyment, are in a hurry to get on with living – like people who know they have short lives ahead of them and eagerly seek to spend every minute on the pleasures of the moment. The trees bud and grow thick with leaves in a single week. There is no more eloquent statement of their endurance than the fact that if you cut stakes from these trees and remove their leaves, they sometimes produce buds and start growing again.[17]

These several days of spring seemed to have a positive effect on the prisoners of war, and they were more lively than usual as they gathered outside their barracks. During the meeting, as always, opinions were divided. Some thought it prudent to return to Blagoveschensk; others enthusiastically defended the continuation of the journey west.

A Romanian anarchist counseled that we hike through the forest. He bolstered his argument by telling us about the Orochen, a people born and bred in the deepest forest who knew the place like the backs of their hands and could give us help and guidance.[18]

An Austrian, taking a map from his pocket, addressed the crowd as follows:

"I work for the topographical section of the partisan army. I've given a lot of thought, and gathered a lot of information, on this matter of how we get to Europe. The railroad has been destroyed. North of the railroad, there is no road, and, even if it existed, we would risk running into detachments of Whites or Reds or Japanese. I assume we want to avoid fighting, given that our goal is to get to Europe alive. Going back is also a doubtful proposition. The Japanese have reestablished their military front at Khabarovsk. It is true that by following the Songhua River we could reach Harbin, the capital of Manchuria, but no one knows the color of the régime currently in charge of Harbin. If it's Red, they'll shoot us as Whites, and if it's White, they'll shoot us as Reds. There's only one option available to us: to go westwards."

We listened with much curiosity as he pointed to the map:

"North of us there's neither town nor village, as you can see from the map. This means that we are dealing with virgin forest. There are probably nomads living there, but no one knows where. But look here: two big rivers, the Olekma and the Vitim, run parallel to one another, finally meeting in the River Lena. We would only have to go a few hundred miles to reach the head waters of these rivers. We could then reach the Lena by building rafts. In peacetime there used to be a steamship connection between Irkutsk and Yakutsk; maybe it has not shut down completely. We are only 1500 miles or so from Yakutsk, a small matter for wanderers like ourselves.[19] From Irkutsk, of course, we will travel by express train...."

"But we'll need guns for protection. Where will we get them?" asked a particularly punctilious baker.

"'Through the Primeval Forest with Sticks and Staves' would make a good title for a fantasy novel," someone remarked.

Chapter III — Consultation

"We'd be crazy to travel through the forest with no horses," declared a cavalry officer who evidently couldn't imagine a world without horses.

The comments continued, until there was so much noise that no one could be heard.

"Quiet!" cried the Austrian. "Horses are not absolutely necessary, and we can get hold of guns."

"Where?" demanded three or four doubters noisily. In the ensuing chaos no one could understand anyone.

"Shut up, for God's sake and let me explain. I propose that we send a deputation to Colonel Shilov, the partisan commander (now the president of the D.V.R.[20]) to ask for his help. If he provides it, fine; if not, we lose nothing."

The proponent of the idea, a man called Hohenberg, was chosen, along with me because we were the best speakers of Russian, and clearly Russian was the most suitable language for the negotiations.

The train occupied by the partisan command stood in the railroad station at Kseniovskaya, and in the sole first-class compartment lived Dimitri Shilov, former czarist officer. So we made our way there to ask him for help. The adjutant greeted us with chilly courtesy.[21]

"What do you want, comrades?"

It was immediately apparent that the adjutant was not a member of Russian polite society: even though he himself was drinking tea, he did not invite us to join him. Russian customs being what they were, this was offensive.

"We have an important matter to discuss with the commander in chief."

"He is very busy. Try to solve your problem with the chief of staff," he replied, regarding us with some hostility.

"We can take this matter up only with the commander in chief," we persisted.

Such decisiveness is nowhere more effective than in Russia – a truth that was confirmed once again, when the adjutant, returning a moment later from the inner depths of the train, invited us in with a friendly smile.

"The commander in chief is waiting for you."

Entering the compartment, we were surprised at the intimate arrangement of the furniture, and we felt a certain aesthetic pleasure as we sat down on the softly upholstered chairs. Shilov, of middle height, with almond eyes and a faced tanned the color of copper, received us. We saw immediately that he was not a pure-blooded Russian, but a rather exotic mixture of Russian, Mongolian and Buryat blood. I was struck, having lived for a long time outside the society of women, by his almost feminine beauty. He spoke politely, and his melodious voice was of a kind that created immediate friendship.

We explained everything to him in detail – our sufferings, plans, and hopes.

"Your Excellency, you have fought for freedom against Japanese oppression: you have to understand us. We also have some rights to a free life. We ask for your permission to leave, and, for a few... weapons."

The commander in chief listened attentively.

"Unfortunately I can do nothing without staff approval, but I will give you my final response within 24 hours."

We hoped for a miracle and actually got one. On the afternoon of the following day, the commander summoned us back. He was very friendly and immediately ordered that a samovar be prepared, to provide us with tea during the meeting. He asked after our well-being. As we drank our sugarless tea, he asked:

Chapter III — Consultation

"Are any of you capable of preparing new maps?"

"Absolutely," I replied self-confidently. "We are former officers, and drawing maps is child's play for people like us."

"That's wonderful, because your plan to avoid the front by moving through the forest is brilliant. Yours is not the only uncertain situation, believe me: ours, that of the partisan army, is extremely uncertain too. If the Japanese attack us, I myself have no idea where we would withdraw. To the east, around Khabarovsk, the way is barred by the Japanese trenches, and to the west lies the taiga, where we could all starve to death. To be captured by the Japanese is not at all to my taste. That is why we are also seriously considering your plan. Our army is currently in a miserable situation. Our soldiers have only a few dozen cartridges each and there is nowhere to turn for further supplies. None the less, we want to make a real effort to support your project. I know how cunning and resourceful prisoners of war can be. We too are interested in finding a way out, and so we will provide you with the wherewithal to put your plan in motion. Choose twenty or thirty men and we will equip them. Intendent Gruzinski already has orders to that effect. In return, we ask you to draw up and prepare a good map of the route you take, so that we can follow it if necessary."

Needless to say, to have the chance to carry out our plan we were ready to promise not just the preparation of a map, but entire mountains of gold.

Returning to our quarters, we celebrated our triumph with our fellows.

CHAPTER IV
Choice

*Wherein are described a few of the characters
with whom we will live, or, in some cases, die.*

The hard work began. It was very important that we choose wisely the members of the expedition who were to head into the forest, and equip them as well as possible. Polar travelers and African explorers would surely have smiled at the ineptness of our preparations and the modesty of our goals.

Some two or three hundred former prisoners of war were living in the area. All, without exception, were eager to participate in any new venture, regardless of possible hardship, since their present condition seemed so miserable that any change would be an improvement.

Given that only twenty or thirty people could take part in the expedition, our main criteria for participation were the right personality, an ability to work hard, and certain specific skills, along with other characteristics. Friendship was also a factor: a friendly face sometimes stood a better chance of selection. In our group there was great diversity of nationality, age, knowledge, social standing, education – and these all influenced the choice.

First in line for selection were two Austrians, Dolfi and Sepi, both of them partisans, who had lived in the forest for the past two years.

How could this be? Austrians in virgin forest? As we all know, the aforementioned nation lives largely in Vienna and its suburbs, where

Chapter IV *Choice*

the one thing missing appears to be primeval forest. But such was the case: both had lived in the forest.

Dolfi and Sepi were prisoners of war. In 1918, many prisoners of war were recruited into the Red Army. When, at the end of the summer of 1918, the Whites launched a further offensive in Siberia, most of the Red Army was destroyed, and only a small part of it succeeded in escaping into the mountains and the forest. Siberia, despite colonization by outsiders, is inhabited only along railroads and rivers: the greater part of central Siberia consists of thousands upon thousands of uninhabited square miles made up exclusively of virgin forest, named *taiga*. When the Red regime collapsed, Dolfi and Sepi took to the forest. At first, when they grew hungry they bought bread and other provisions from the inhabitants of the nearest village, using gold or silver. They had gold until the supply at the Chita bank ran out (the so-called "anarchist company" cleaned out the bank in Chita in 1918). The villagers, despite severe penalties, helped the partisans with food. If a villager was found guilty of helping a Bolshevik, the entire village was burned and its inhabitants exterminated – men, women and children – and, at the time, people made no distinction between Red Guards and Bolsheviks. Another way of obtaining needed provisions was to derail a train and steal its contents.

When the gold ran out and the armies of the Whites and the Japanese had mercilessly exterminated a few villages, the life of an outlaw became more or less untenable. They were pursued like mad dogs: good Cossack hunting parties could shoot twenty or thirty of them a day. Sepi and Dolfi suffered terribly together during those long days and months. Such suffering forged a strong bond of friendship between them.

"So, tell us. What was the worst of your adventures?" I once asked in curiosity, during a conversation about the terrors and perils of the *taiga*.

"When we ate our comrade Hans."

Dolfi dug Sepi in the ribs.

"Aren't you ashamed to talk about such things?" Dolfi whispered, but Sepi none the less quietly continued his story.

"At the time there were ten of us living together. To begin with, there were thirty in the group, but death with its healthy appetite consumed the rest. Hunger tore at our guts: we had nothing to put in our bellies. We had eaten the last remains of a horse and we were already chewing desperately on its hooves and hair. The effects of hunger turned Hans crazy. We could hardly send him to the hospital, because there was no hospital to send him to. In fact if anyone got sick in the forest, or got wounded, there was no help for him, and without a doctor he simply closed his eyes and went to sleep forever. So what could we do for our unfortunate comrade? We were hungry too, and so ... we ate him. As we ate, we talked of his and our unhappy fate. Later we ate someone else, but he had it coming to him: we punished him because he was guilty. He stole food from our provisions.... But he tasted better than they did. Right, Sepi?"

I have the courage to tell this terrible story only to throw some light on the abyss into which war pushes us so-called human beings.

Anyway, for an expedition through virgin forest you can hardly limit your choice to gentlemen — and Sepi and Dolfi had other important qualifications. Having lived in the forest for two years, they had experience, and for such a risk-filled journey we needed people like that. When we asked whether they would agree to go on this difficult trip, they said that they would be pleased to, but only if they did not have to work.

"For two years we lived in the forest without working and we have no wish to work again as long as we live," said Dolfi.

"We don't deserve it," added Sepi.

Chapter IV — Choice

After much discussion we decided that they would not have to participate in the most onerous work....

We wanted to prepare for all eventualities. What would happen if our provisions ran out? Where would we find food?

"We'll hunt and fish," it was agreed. "There are plenty of animals in the forest – bison, bear, deer, wild boar. The rivers are full of fish."

"We won't die of hunger," I said confidently. "Our job is to line up people who know about hunting and fishing."

We soon found a hunter. One of our number announced that his peacetime occupation was that of poacher on the estates of Count Esterházi. With much rejoicing he was chosen officer-in-charge-of-hunting.

And so on... In fact, every member of our expedition would merit a page or two about his character or lack of it. As for occupations, the group could be categorized as follows: one idealistic lawyer, two normal agriculturists, one alcoholic agriculturist, two carpenters, one office worker (but with the soul of a poet), two students, one domestic servant, two locksmiths, one active non-commissioned officer, one tailor, and several farm laborers.

The reader will probably immediately note the lack of women. In fact, we planned to travel without women, but at the last moment a Russian woman, romantically linked to one of the prisoners of war, announced that she had decided to accompany us. We protested in vain, and in vain we described the expected terrors of the journey.

"I have one life and one death," she said, and, shaving her hair and putting on trousers, she followed her lover. (In the interest of full disclosure, I should add that she was eight years his senior.)

Having carefully made our preparations, after two or three days we had everything we needed – from medicines to needle and thread. The army supply officers gave us everything they had, but unfortunately they did not have much. The biggest problem was the question of horses. We had asked for twenty-five of them, and the agreement was that we would return them when we reached the river. Although the partisan leadership had assigned the horses to us, we did not actually have them, since it was no easy task to convince partisans to part with horses. The younger members of the expedition wanted to set out anyway – on foot. The older members, and those with partisan experience, insisted that horses were essential for forest travel. So we had two parties: the horse-supporters and the horseless. The weather favored the former: it rained and rained and rained, night and day.

"So, go without horses," the horse-lovers mockingly suggested. "Though God knows how you will carry your provisions. Even without such burdens, you'll probably drown in the mud."

CHAPTER V
First Obstacles

*In this chapter the author shows how continued progress,
like most things in life, takes longer than expected.*

The special train stopped. Our journey would begin from here. We jumped down and quickly gathered our provisions. Parallel to the railroad ran what was apparently a small river, the Cherniy Uryum. The plan called for our crossing it.[22] On the map it was shown as a mere stream, with nothing to hinder our getting across.[23] In reality, however, hindrances abounded. We had intended to move forward and cover a few miles immediately, but we had not gone a hundred yards before we found that our little river was in fact a noisy, boiling, powerful torrent.

"We'll never get across that monster," cried the tallest of our party, whom we called Big Mouth, a title he was later to show he richly deserved. We were all quickly convinced that we could not just take the river in our stride — and there was no bridge. There was nothing to do but to set up our tent, which we did, next to a pond alongside the railroad. We had a small waterproof tent, big enough for ten people. The rain continued serenely, steadily, without interruption. We were all of us already so wet that our whole bodies felt like slimy, slippery sponges.

Dolfi came up with a good idea to deal with the rain.

"You can take pieces of tree bark and use them as protection."

We began. At first our efforts were clumsy, but with the help of sharpened sticks we made better progress. The bark was very effective: we were protected from the constant rain. But our spirits stayed the same – sour and uncertain. The stripped and naked trees, sole witnesses to our plight, looked like huge, mysterious candles.

What could we do? What could possibly help? A few hundred paces away this huge roaring mountain river barred our way. How could we reach the other side? No one had an answer. We turned to the local railroad workers for advice, but they only repeated what we already knew, namely that there was no bridge. The nearest, in fact, was 100 miles away to the south. The river was as high as it was only because of the unusual amount of rain that we had been having: normally even a child could get across.

A thousand times we asked the same question: "How can we get to the other side?"

"When the water goes down," they replied.

"And if it rains for a month?"

"Then you wait for a month," was the laconic reply.

As Goethe put it, we resist the gods in vain.[24] We sensed a certain truth in Goethe's observation as we contemplated the steady and incessant rain. Most people in the group were very upset, and some of them wanted to try to cross anyway, despite the obstacles; others hoped for some new proposal or counted on a change in the weather. Unfortunately, although it was already June, the river was so cold that you could not even keep your hand in it for very long, and it was hopeless to think of any prolonged activity in the water.

The only, and also most comfortable, solution appeared to be to wait.

The following dawn brought further disagreeable news. Excited shouts and cries broke the early morning silence. The person in charge of the horses tremblingly recounted that two dead bodies were lying

Chapter V *First Obstacles*

on the railroad track: two of our horses had been struck by a train during the night. Among my readers may be some who have themselves experienced the value of a horse in territory of this kind – as a friend and comrade as well as a worker – and they will readily appreciate our dejection. If four people rather than two horses had died, we would have been less distressed. How could such a thing have happened? We could only wonder. I have already mentioned that there was a real mixture of people in our group. Among them were city dwellers who had never even seen a horse from close up and who, needless to say, knew nothing at all about looking after them. The former cavalry officer, in charge of the horse department, put out an official decree: "All horses must be tied together, with their hoofs properly hobbled, and only then may they be put out to pasture."

Our minister of horses showed us how to hobble horses to prevent them from running away. But several of us had no experience in such matters, being acquainted only with the profound philosophical truth that it is not a good idea to pick up a horse's hoof if you are not insured against kicks.

Probably the horses had not been properly roped together, the rope had fallen off, and the horses had wandered away in various directions. Two horses were on the rails when the train approached quite slowly. An approaching train in the middle of a forest can, with its shining eyes, mesmerize people, let alone such horses, which, as far as we could tell, had never even seen a train. Anyway the tragedy had happened, irreparably, and the resulting pool of blood testified as much. We cursed our bad luck, but there was nothing we could do to change it.

Despite the pouring rain, a small group of us went down to the river to see if anyone could come up with any bright ideas on what to do next. By throwing stones across, we tried to establish its width. The answer: something over forty yards.

While we were talking, one of the farmers explained that during the war he had served with a group of workers responsible for building a bridge, and he had seen how quickly it could be done. He laid out for us a simple means of construction: what we had to do was build a floating bridge, without a foundation in the river bed. We could construct the framework on the bank and, as each section was completed, push it into the river. If the framework were longer than the width of the river, the other end would attach itself to the far side and the bridge would be ready for use.

We only half understood the plan, but he gave such convincing explanations, with the aid of drawings, sketches, and matchsticks, that after a time we were converted into true believers.

That evening, there was much discussion about the plan; but the general mood was bad, and the pessimists prevailed on all fronts. We established very firm procedures for the night, setting up a guard roster so that we could avoid any further disagreeable surprises. On the bridge-building plan opinions were divided.

The skeptics maintained that it would be best to wait for the water to recede.

"But if it rains for a month, does that mean we'll wait for a month?" some of the group asked. A majority decided to start work.

"*Everyone* has to work!" cried Big Mouth.

"Yes, we need a requirement that everyone do work duty," added others.

Only Sepi and Dolfi were excluded from the requirement. They were to serve as cooks.

My assigned guard duty began at midnight. It gave me time to think. Would I ever sleep on pillows and mattress again, I asked myself?

The camp fire barely glimmered, and seemed about to die with the damp – like my own hopes.

CHAPTER VI
The Crossing

In which the reader will learn about efforts so great that they might move mountains.

Four o'clock the following morning was the appointed wake-up time. The only earlier riser was the sun. The trees were heavy with rain: if you touched them, the leaves released a minor torrent. The ground was sodden, saturated with water.

We set to work energetically on our difficult assignment, and soon the silence of the virgin *taiga* was shattered by the sound of our saws and axes. Some of the group had never really experienced physical labor, but they made up in enthusiasm and ambition what they lacked in skill. With any physical task of this kind the tools should be entrusted to those with the necessary experience; the job goes more easily that way and you get double the success with half the effort. I must confess that some of us knew nothing of such principles of economy, and the skilled members of the group smiled disdainfully as they watched our idealistic lawyer wield his ax. In fact there was no shortage of derogatory comments all round.

With what was truly a superhuman effort we succeeded in carrying the trees that we had felled, each 45 feet in length, to the river's edge. Although some thirteen or fourteen people carried each tree, we often felt as though our shoulders would break under the weight. We attached three long beams to one another, giving us the required length.

We were acutely aware of the lack of proper technical equipment. We were short of metal nails, for example, and so we used drills and wooden dowels. After three days, working twelve hours a day, we were finally able to admire our collective handiwork: the framework for the bridge lay ready on the bank.

During this tiring work, we paid little attention to the weather. It was nothing if not varied – one minute bright blue sky and brilliant sun, and the next heavy downpours. The weather was like some grand lady changing her clothes ten times a day.

But such things went unheeded: we were interested only in the bridge. If our plan succeeds, and if the bridge is sturdy enough and long enough, our first major obstacle will be overcome... And a first success will bring others...

A great deal of careful preparation was required when it came time to push the bridge into the water. Everyone was mobilized for the occasion. The commander of the partisans came in person to visit us and provided twenty Cossacks to assist. Our plan was to slide the framework into the water by means of a slipway of smooth logs.

Our agricultural expert, the author of the plan, gave the orders.

"Use stones and ropes to anchor the front part of the bridge! Hold this cable."

"Why aren't you working?"

"I'm working, but the Cossacks aren't."

"The rope's going to break!"

"Three people, over here!"

Commands and counter-commands could be heard on all sides, and we held our breaths to see how the current would carry the bridge to the other side. Fearing that the bridge would not be long enough, we had attached thick cables to the middle section and only very slowly

Chapter VI — The Crossing

allowed it to turn in the river. Any schoolboy can tell you that wood is lighter than water and floats on the surface – but in our case things did not work according to the textbook. The bridge became a powerful obstacle in the way of the flowing mass of water and we were amazed to see that its central section was actually pushed downwards by the current. We could see only the front and rear sections above the water: the middle was a foot or two beneath the surface.

This made it impossible to proceed further. All our hard work and effort seemed in vain. The only way of saving the situation was to raise the middle section by supporting it from underneath – but the icy water prevented us from proceeding.

"Failure seldom walks alone, and he who goes to bed with Mistress Care also rises with her," says a Buryat proverb. Our failure left us morally and physically depressed. Soon, fate dealt us a further blow.

When the partisan commander saw the failure of our plan, he announced he was withdrawing his earlier offer. Knowing that we had lost two horses, he also asked for the other horses back. As for the members of the group, they could head off in any direction they fancied, or they could join the partisan army as workers.[25]

Among ourselves, we were very upset at this further setback, but we knew we had to keep our self-control and attempt to negotiate a change of heart on the commander's part. In subsequent discussion it became clear that the matter went deeper: his staff had completely changed their original plan. Because of the threat from the Japanese, they now wanted to open up the forest route for entire regiments. A group of Russian cartographers would draw the necessary maps and laborers would prepare the way along the route selected. So we could sign on as ordinary laborers if we wanted to, and our job would be to make the first twenty-five miles accessible to wheeled vehicles. After that, we would have the right to move forward through the forest on our own.

"But we can't work without horses."

"Who will carry the provisions?" added one of our negotiators.

"Even the partisans have no horses," replied the commander. "Our hussars have to fight without them."

After much discussion, he never the less left us ten horses.

"If you don't like my decision, you're free to turn back."

We now saw how committed everyone was to our expedition into the forest: only five people opted to return.

These five of course tried to convince the rest of us.

"Your plan is total fantasy! It'll never succeed, and you'll all kill yourselves."

But their words made no impression on our determination.

Years ago, I saw an American play called *Inundation*. When people had lost all hope of saving their lives, they became friendly, likable, polite. I must say that in my experience proximity to death doesn't seem to improve people. For most, self-love seems to be the prevailing emotion. I well remember that, even though the returnees knew that we were playing with death and that the smallest of things might save lives, two of them "forgot" to return several tools, and only when we sent a group of riders to intercept them did we succeed in recovering everything they had taken.

Our life was eventful indeed, and every moment brought a new surprise. When we looked out at the river next morning, the bridge had simply ceased to exist. During the night, the current had grown so much that the force of the water had snapped the three metal cables and carried it away. We later heard that our bridge-building effort actually destroyed the real bridge a hundred miles to the south.[26] Not only was the bridge of no use to us, but it actually caused harm to others.

Chapter VI — The Crossing

The episode ended and new work began, but now under the guidance of the Russian expert. We tried to build an ordinary bridge, with wood that had to be transported from a place nearby, but this new construction also failed because the rapid current sank the wood every time.

Meanwhile, boats arrived. Wonderful! We started on a pontoon bridge. On one occasion we actually reached the other side, but during our return the waves overwhelmed the pontoons and only after much effort did we succeed in saving the boats. We kept at it for ten days. Finally, we succeeded with a modified plan. We fixed a boat to a metal cable attached to both banks, and we used the boat to transport our provisions. To get the wagons across, we took them apart, and we made the horses swim.

One small misfortune, at least for the gastronomes among us, was the loss of our favorite calf, which jumped out of the boat and ran off into the forest.

CHAPTER VII
Pursuit

This chapter shows that being the object of hostile pursuit sometimes has its agreeable side.

So we reached the other bank. In the larger scheme of things, this was only a small success, but it meant a lot to us, and it helped us to look on our adventurous undertaking with a little more optimism. In fact sometimes our mood was downright cheerful. It felt good to rest in the tent at the end of the day, with green branches burning in the center of our circle to protect us from the mosquitoes. We lay with closed eyes on our grass pallets and talked or joked or listened to our idealist lawyer make grand speeches about the meaning of life or the mechanical and spiritual perception of the world. On such occasions, even the forest looked better to us, with its bushes, trees, large and small, all in various shades of green. The massive trees, surviving in this environment over hundreds of years, testified to the enduring power of nature.

The richness of the natural world contrasted sharply with our somewhat simple meals. We mostly ate dried, salted fish, with bread. But one morning our agriculturist made a great discovery.

"Look what I've found," he cried enthusiastically. He had come upon mulberries left behind under last year's dead leaves. We had not eaten fruit in a long time and the sour berries tasted delicious. When the order came to collect mulberries for our common kitchen, there was much rejoicing. Such work was altogether easier than sawing, or collecting branches.

Chapter VII — Pursuit

As we gathered mulberries, our student sighed unhappily. "It's a shame that our farming expert couldn't find any sugar or cooking fat while he was about it." And he swallowed down a mouthful of sour fruit.

This episode did not affect the important task of road-building. We worked eleven or twelve hours a day. The night guard woke us every morning at four, and we managed to get to bed at ten each evening. Every day brought new challenges. Building a road across marshland was no child's play.[27] We laid one log in front of another and slowly moved our wagons forward. And those who have never tried it have no idea how difficult it is to yoke horses. Many of us learned, the wrong way, what skill, imagination and cleverness is required. An extremely elaborate collection of straps and ropes was connected to the collars of the horses, and failure to attach them properly had the most unexpected consequences. Every time, something went wrong. And even if the ropes were properly attached, there was always a good chance that a wheel would fly off an axle because the load was too heavy for it...

The horses lived a privileged life, and it was more than a person's life was worth if his carelessness caused a horse to break a foot or suffer a wound on the back.

From one day to the next, the flies and mosquitoes made our life less and less tenable. Every hour of the day and night seemed to have its particular species of fly. In the morning and at night the chief problem was mosquitoes, in the middle of the day enormous flies, and in the afternoon swarms of tiny ones. And their numbers were beyond all measure. Occasionally they attacked us with such fury that, despite our attempts to defend ourselves, they literally filled our mouths and eyes. We had no mosquito nets, and the sheets that we created for ourselves were not very effective; the bites made our heads swell up like pumpkins.

The horses suffered even more than we did. By flailing about with our arms we were able to drive the various blood-sucking flies away from us, but our poor horses were helpless, and their tails simply could not fend off the millions of flies and mosquitoes. The gray horse, for example, turned completely black with flies and dried blood from their bites. Every time we stopped to rest, we built a big fire of green sticks to protect the horses with the smoke.

The horses, wisely, sensed its positive effect and huddled round the fire so closely that they almost burned their heads off.

We were eager to finish the work we had undertaken as quickly as possible, fearing that winter would arrive and put paid to all our plans. We built the road where the trees grew least densely. The ground varied: in the mountains it was stony and unyielding and in the valleys it was wet and marshy.[28] The marshy land was a particular hindrance, and in spite of all our efforts we covered only some two or three miles a day. Of course, our responsibility was "to make the road passable," and "make passable" is a very elastic term. So, eleven days later we judged our work complete. We reported as much to the Russian *desyatnik* (project manager) and, given that in Russia it is usual to ask for something, we asked for food and clothing.

"You call that road ready? Horses couldn't use it, let alone wagons."

"We've been working really hard, and *our* wagons made it. If ours did, others will too."

Finally the project manager said that he would make a full report to the partisan command, but that he did not think we would be given permission to leave.

We already knew what "making a report" meant: a new round of negotiations, and further delay and loss of time, possibly lasting months. Several of us were extremely agitated at the manager's response.

"I've said many times that the Russians have been cheating us and always will do," said the former domestic servant.

Chapter VII — Pursuit

"We should have left long ago, but our 'esteemed leaders' have always talked us out of it," cried Big Mouth.

We had little to lose. We took stock of our provisions and decided. We had four sacks of bread, a hundred or so pounds of rice and flour, some 35 pounds of salt. In reserve we had our horses, and we were sure that we would find animals and fish in the forest. We calculated sixty pounds of food for each person, and we figured that, used carefully, it would last for a month and a half. We also had nine guns, and sufficient axes, saws, drills, ropes, and other items. We were equipped with a compass and a large enough supply of such expendable items as nails, matches, ammunition, and money.

And we were all of us healthy, full of life. It did not take us long to decide to leave without permission.

Two of us agreed to be responsible for riding back and breaking off communication with the world by cutting the telegraph wires.[29] The rest of us set to work with feverish speed. We did not want to take the wagons, and so to replace them we made our own panniers. The travelers divided into ten groups, each of two or three people, responsible for one horse and for assisting it as needed. Everything packed on the horses was declared common property. If anyone decided to carry something on his own back, that was his own affair.

Morning had not yet broken when our sweating envoys returned and we set out in a long caravan. We felt proud as the well-laden horses moved off, attended by our careful comrades and greeted by the resplendent trees, bowing to us in the wind as we passed.

Finding the way was easy. We followed the edge of a stream that flowed down into the Olekma River.[30] Though we moved as quickly as possible, there were frequent stops, on the prearranged signal, a single shot. Ropes came undone; straps broke; a saddle was poorly positioned and required repacking a load.

We had traveled a bare six hours when three shots rang out. This was our agreed-upon danger signal. We all ran – except Sepi and Dolfi, who stayed with the horses – in the direction of the signal. The thick undergrowth made it difficult to run, and we struggled forward without even thinking about the nature of the danger that might await us. When we reached the spot we found a collection of people, colleagues and strangers, in smiling embrace.

What had happened? Where had these strangers come from? In a matter of minutes, all was clear. The commander of the partisans, when he learned that we had left, ordered the Cossacks posted along the river to pursue us and confiscate our supplies. But the boat was not in position and only six Cossacks succeeded in swimming across the river with their horses. Among them were three European Russians who had long been looking for a way of returning home. This seemed like a good opportunity. They had volunteered to pursue us, but their actual aim was to get home.

"Allow us," said the oldest, whose hair hung down to his eyes, "to come along with you, and everything that we have is yours."

"Hooray," we all cried with a single voice. "Long live our Cossack brothers!"

The arrival of these three Cossacks was fortunate indeed. Three good horses and guns were a valuable addition, though we had three additional stomachs to feed.

But now we made good progress. We reassigned the luggage and relieved our horses. Late in the evening we halted. To celebrate our successful day's march, we distributed a double portion of rice. We built big fires. As we sat there, our faces bronzed by the sun and our profiles etched in the red firelight, we looked like so many Red Indians.

After a three-day march, and without further incident, we reached the Olekma River.[31]

CHAPTER VIII
Among the Orochen

The reader learns that there are savages not only in Europe but also in Eastern Siberia.

Up to this point in our journey, we had sometimes had the impression that human knowledge, or judgment, or will, or self-sacrifice, were ultimately useless: in the battle against the power and play of nature no human ever wins. Whether there is sunshine or rain may seem a matter of little importance, but in fact it influences the lives of millions.

Whenever the Olekma River was mentioned, we expressed a certain nervousness. The map showed it as much larger than the Chornoi Uryum, and we calculated that it would take us at least three days to cross.

Quite the reverse.

We were cursed at the Uryum, but blessed at the Olekma.

For days we had had tranquil, beautiful weather. The sky was a majestic blue. Mister Sun shone uninterruptedly. There was no rain, and the lack of rain kept the river low. The current was fast, but, like a docile child, it made little noise with its waves.

Reaching the Olekma, we had not even unloaded the horses before two of our party tested the depth and speed of the river.

"I bet my today's bread supply that we can't wade across," cried the student, ever the pessimist.

"It'll take us weeks of work to get over," added another.

But this time the pessimists were wrong. The river was no deeper than about four feet and could be crossed by men and beasts without any special preparation.[32]

To withstand the force of the current, we took stout sticks in our hands. Some people tied themselves together. We set out without delay, and, tired but happy, quickly reached the soft, velvety sand on the other bank.

To celebrate this lucky day, we decided to take a day off and clean ourselves up. We really deserved the day of rest, and the ablutions were necessary too. In our present condition, we could hardly have presented ourselves in the average drawing room. Our clothes were torn. Our shoes, which just a few weeks ago were stout and strong, were now scarcely usable. Our shirts were half black with dried sweat. Our heads were covered with long hair and beards. My readers, living in normal circumstances, have never felt the pleasure of removing a shirt unwashed for three weeks and putting on a clean one. Most of us mended our clothes or cleaned ourselves up while four of us rode off on horseback to look for the Orochen.

The Orochen! We had heard the name many times. We knew that in the vicinity of the Olekma River there lived native nomads of that name.[33] The question was how to find them. As soon as we reached the river, we fired several shots into the air to attract their attention, but without result. We felt that if we could find them the results could turn out to be very positive for us. We might obtain food from them, or they could serve as guides. So we waited with much curiosity to see whether our Orochen hunt would prove successful. Three or four hours had already passed and our comrades had not returned.

"Clearly something has happened to them," we heard from one group – a remark made this time not by our pessimistic student but by one of the farmers.

"Perhaps the Orochen have caught them and killed them," someone else suggested.

"The Orochen are the nicest people in the world," said Dolfi, a participant in this conversation, in their defense; "And Sepi won't let them kill him," he added confidently – a confidence not without justification for someone who had lived the previous two years in the forest.

"Probably they've found nothing and they're embarrassed to come back empty-handed," was the general conclusion.

These discussions had their own rather interesting character. We used three languages: German, Hungarian, and Russian. As our main international auxiliary language we mostly used Russian, but hand gestures also played a significant role.[34]

It was late afternoon by the time our comrades returned. We heard their shouts in the distance.

"We've found them!"

At once we surrounded the returnees and bombarded them with questions.

"Where did you meet them? When? Who? What do they look like?"

"How do they live? Is it true that they only have reindeer? Will they guide us? Were they frightened of you?"

Needless to say, it was not easy to reply to all these questions.

Our comrades, it seems, had wandered around for four hours before they came upon an Orochen village – men, women, and children. The Orochen were much surprised to see foreigners. Only one of them had ever had contact with Russians. So it was difficult for our comrades to make themselves understood. After much explanation, they finally grasped that we were travelers on our way to the west and that we had lots of provisions. For this last reason they at once agreed to come and barter with us. Our comrades were to ride ahead to tell us, and to prepare the horses: the Orochen would come by reindeer, and the horses might be frightened.

"They're here!" cried the person on guard duty. And into sight came a fascinating procession of some thirty or forty people. They were riding reindeer. The reindeer were very delicate, skittish, and graceful animals, some of them with antlers of as many as sixteen branches. The men rode singly on the reindeer, the women together with two or three children. Both men and women wore similar deerskin garments.

In appearance, there was no great difference between the men and the women, though I must confess that the women's clothes looked less worn than those of the men. They were recognizably of Mongolian extraction. Their narrow, slanted eyes, prominent cheek bones and flat noses made them very much like the races of Eastern Siberia, the Yakuts and the Buryats. The children were of poor stature and many of them had hunched backs.

Our meeting was marked by open and lively enthusiasm on both sides. We were particularly taken with the reindeer and the children, and after a few minutes became fast friends. To show off our riches, we set about arranging a display, and half an hour later laid it before them. It contained a hundred and ten objects. They were impressed by everything, and particularly liked our pocket telescope, the cigarette lighter, and our lawn handkerchiefs. Our little market was a great success. The Orochen were all over us to exchange their possessions for ours, and they invited us to visit their village. So we decided to extend our time off and pay our hospitable new friends a visit.

CHAPTER IX
A Visit to an Orochen Village

The reader with no interest in Orochen villages need not read this chapter, in which the author describes certain characteristics of the nomadic life.

Where a little river joined the Olekma, near rich pastureland, we found the Orochen village.[35] Do not imagine anything very impressive under the name of village: the entire community consisted of only four tents, constructed of birch branches with birch bark as covering. The tents stood next to one another like so many white cones. Each was no more than fifteen or twenty feet in diameter, and in each tent some ten or a dozen people lived, making up a single family. Four or five families in turn made up a tribe, and each tribe lived separately from the others. It was one of these tribes that we had found.

"Their tents are charming!"

"But how do they manage in minus forty-degree weather?"

"Have you ever had reindeer milk?"

Questions like these could be heard on all sides as we approached the village. Close to the village was an area of reindeer pasture, with three or four hundred reindeer and their young. The deer were amazingly docile, and you could easily catch them or touch and stroke them. But our horses were afraid of these antlered creatures and had no wish to make friends with them.

A few of us went into one of the tents.

"Sit and eat!" said the oldest Orochen, pointing to chairs set up in the tent. They entertained us heartily, with reindeer meat followed by reindeer milk. Europeans have difficulty understanding how people can live without bread. We of course knew otherwise from the Japanese, who eat boiled rice rather than bread. The Orochen had bread to be sure, but they made it not with flour, but with reindeer curds. Following the meal, wishing to thank them for their hospitality, we gave them cigarettes. Immediately even the smallest child wanted to smoke, as we discovered a few hours later when they started looking for cigarettes in our pockets. We played a lot with the children, having been deprived of their company for many years.

That night brought new worries. The reindeer herd came too close to our horses, and the horses panicked, breaking their halters and running off. We searched for them all night, and came up with all kinds of fantastic plans to recover them. Everyone was pressed into service. Partly on horseback and partly on foot, we looked for them in all directions. The search was made all the more difficult by the swarms of insects, which hardly gave us a chance to breathe. We feared that perhaps the horses had swum back to the other bank of the river.

Next morning we alerted the Orochen, promising them big rewards if they found the horses. Without horses we would be lost, and so with understandable apprehension we awaited the results of their efforts. The Orochen set off from the place where the horses were tethered and then followed their tracks. They did not take long to find them. We rewarded our saviors generously, with two pounds of salt. This was a really princely gift, because the Orochen had no salt. Not only were the Orochen themselves hungry for it, but so were the reindeer. If you just put a grain or two of salt on your hand, some fifty or sixty reindeer would immediately gather round to lick it off. In fact the animals sought salty things all the time and even started chewing on our backpacks. Urination was downright dangerous because of the reindeer charge it was apt to provoke. While we were out looking for

Chapter IX — A Visit to an Orochen Village

the horses, the reindeer took the opportunity to forage through our possessions. In one backpack a reindeer found, not salt, but a pound of sugar, which one of our number, with great self-control, had been saving up. The reindeer was evidently upset when he found sugar rather than salt, but, what was he to do? He ate it anyway. We could not contain our laughter when our comrade discovered that he had lost in one night the accumulation of a month.

The visit to the Orochen gave our linguists and ethnographers a good opportunity to study a people living and functioning "without culture," as they say in Europe. To understand their customs and habits, they began studying the Orochen language. I was among those who enthusiastically took up the challenge and I became quite proficient in the language, though unfortunately today I can recall none of it. I remember only that *oron* means "reindeer" and *Orocheny* "the reindeer people."

They could not be better named: their whole lives are focused round the reindeer. In fact it is the source of all their happiness. They ride it, eat its meat, drink only reindeer milk, use its hide for clothing, and make thread out of its intestines. In addition to the reindeer, the birch tree is also very important to them, since their tents are made of birch, and they fashion all manner of implements out of its bark. They sew strips of birch bark together to make boats: lightness is essential on rivers that abound in waterfalls.

To a nomadic people, money is of course worthless, and they know only barter. The old Orochen told us that in peacetime there were places along the river where traders came to exchange things, but that since 1915 no one had come. We ordered the individual members of our group not to engage in barter, but some people could not resist the temptation to obtain a sable skin, or the skin of a beaver, or a bison horn. The going rate varied. A white wolf skin cost fifty cigarettes. They proposed twenty squirrel skins for half a pound of salt. For twenty cartridges they gave us a reindeer. We bought three reindeer for the group. For some time we had wanted to have reindeer meat, and so we decided to butcher one of them and put on a grand banquet.

The old Orochen introduced us to the art of butchering a reindeer. Taking an ax, he crept up on the animal and stationed himself behind it. The reindeer stood quite quietly, and with its innocent eyes looked on us as friends, little knowing that its life was about to end. The old man hit its head quite lightly with the blunt side of the ax. He must have hit the so-called medulla oblongata because the deer immediately fell down dead. Like so many vultures attacking a carcass, some of our group seized on the dead animal, sucking its blood and chewing on the raw flesh without waiting to cook it. I had never imagined that, with only the slightest relaxation of social constraints, people could become such animals.

When the reindeer was cut up, the old Orochen showed us why reindeer cannot run for long in the summertime. The dead animal's nose was full of parasites, which hindered its breathing. The parasites lack resistance to the cold and in winter they die. As a result, reindeer can run long distances in winter, covering as much as seventy or seventy-five miles a day. We asked the Orochen to lend us some reindeer as far as the Vitim River, but they refused, saying that in summer reindeer are unsuitable for long journeys. But the old Orochen, as it turned out, agreed to come with us as our guide when we promised to give him our tent.

Next day, he was indeed ready to guide us. He took with him only three pairs of reindeer-skin moccasins.

"You don't need much when you travel," he said in the Orochen language. The old man set out, and our caravan followed behind.

CHAPTER X
In the Forest

If the reader is interested, he can read in this chapter about the so-called "virgin forest."

Led by our Orochen guide, we were supposed to cover fourteen miles a day, requiring some twelve hours on the march.[36] In fact we seldom met this expectation, and at the start of the day tended to lose time. Something always happened to slow us down and force a change in the day's program. When the call to arms came to us each morning, with a shout for us all to get up, people always wanted "just a couple of minutes more" and lay there pretending to sleep.

The person on night duty always prepared breakfast. Indian fakirs could not eat more simply than we did. Breakfast consisted of boiled water and a few pieces of biscuit. We called the boiled water tea, because occasionally we added a tea leaf or two. We had long forgotten that proper tea was served in some places with sugar and rum...

We were always delighted to receive our daily ration of dried bread, no more than four or five ounces. With what anticipation we waited each morning for the moment when it was handed out! We couldn't bring ourselves to eat it immediately, looking at it and savoring the various pieces with our eyes, and using every trick imaginable to try to make our portions last longer.

Some sucked at it first. Others, after chewing it, kept it in their mouths for several minutes to prolong the pleasure, and only then swallowed it down. Bread distribution always took place under the tightest control and in the presence of our most trusted members. But the most trusted among us were in turn watched suspiciously by everyone else.

After breakfast the serious work began. Getting the horses ready each morning required careful attention. We had made the panniers ourselves, and, accordingly, they were less than perfect, often requiring improvement and repair. A rope would break, or a horse's back get cut – and if a horse was wounded, its load had to be divided among the healthy ones.

A strong bond was created between the horses and their grooms, so that when the loads had to be redistributed, no one wanted his horse to carry a heavier burden, and attempts at redistribution were accompanied by shouts, protests and curses on all sides.

"They're trying to destroy my horse. It can barely carry the load it already has, and now they're adding a bag of biscuit," angrily muttered Kiss, one of our chief horse handlers.

"My horse is nothing but skin and bone, and you want it to carry still more? Have you no heart?" Our poacher pointed to his horse, which did indeed look quite unhappy. Finally, all of the extra load was given to the horse belonging to the idealist lawyer. Both horse and lawyer bore their burden with silent resignation.

Little by little, the party divided into two groups. There were first-class citizens and second-class ones. In the first class were those who knew how to look after horses, and, in the second, those who, like me, did not spend enough time in the stables in their youth and had not become horse experts.

"Of course, they don't teach such things in universities," said Big Mouth sarcastically, seeing our lack of skill. He was always angry at intellectuals...

Chapter X — In the Forest

After a clash of opinions of greater or lesser intensity, the party moved off on its day's march. If nothing intervened to prevent us, we proceeded without stopping to rest for some four hours. Climbing hills was tiring, and the valleys were full of marshes, so it was difficult to say which were worse – hills or valleys. In the valleys we had to jump from one tuft of grass to the next, if we wished to avoid getting our shoes full of water.

"It's a pity I wasn't born a mountain goat," one of our farmers sighed after missing his footing and crawling painfully out of the water.

But one cannot escape fate: we tried in vain to stay dry. After an hour or two's march, pond still followed pond, and stream followed stream. If in a given location we could not pick out a path along fallen trees, we simply waded into the water without removing shoes or trousers and continued our journey soaked to the skin.

The mountains were three thousand feet high or a little more, and the views from their summits were sometimes truly majestic. Even a trip to the cinema would show you no better. But we were in no mood to appreciate the beauties of nature. On an empty stomach one is no aesthete. Wearily we dragged ourselves forward, always looking to see whether we had crossed the watershed, because if the streams began to flow in the opposite direction, that meant that we had passed the highest point in the mountains.

As we marched we drank fresh stream water, as much as four or five liters in the course of a morning. Then in the middle of the day, covered in sweat, we lay on the grass for a mid-day rest. Our cooks were Sepi and Dolfi, who had originally received this exalted office as a privilege. It had become a burden, because they now had to cook as well as walk. Accordingly they proposed a new division of labor, with them giving directions while others performed the more menial tasks.

Lunch was very simple, consisting of gruel or rice. We varied our menu so that if we had tea and gruel at noon, in the evening we cooked rice, and if there was rice for lunch, we had gruel in the evening. We cooked everything with water, because we had no oil or fat. But our appetites were always good, and we licked the plates clean.

We were very careful in the selection of our camping place each evening. We had run out of oats long since, and so without good pasture our weak horses would not be able to carry their loads.

Lack of grass, water and dry wood sometimes forced us to continue our march despite our eagerness to rest; occasionally abundant pasture caused us to cut the march short in the early afternoon.

New perspectives came to us not only from our natural surroundings but also from our guide, the old Orochen. With his sharp intelligence he guided us so skillfully through the dense trees and rivers and mountains. Sometimes in the evenings, having built a big fire to protect us against both the cold (the nights were already chilly) and the insects, we talked in our rather interesting mixture of languages.

"In a few weeks, it will be winter," said someone shivering.

"True, but we Orochen like the winter," said the old man proudly. "Summer is an ugly and unhappy time. Nothing grows but the grass. The bugs won't leave us alone. The heat of the day slows people down. We like the winter – the clean fresh air, the hunting season."

"But how can you live in tents in the winter?" we asked.

"Look at our lovely animals, the reindeer. Their skins protect us against the winter. Their welfare takes a lot of our attention, but rewards us with so many useful things."

"Are you happy with your life?" we asked on occasion.

"Why not? The Orochen are the most noble people in the world. You cannot compare us with the Yakuts or the Buryats. Among us no one is dishonest. Our storehouses are full of dried meat; our tools, our skins, are free; there are no locks and keys in the forest, or on the trees, at heights a man can reach. No one steals, and no one is punished."[37]

Chapter X   *In the Forest*

"But what if someone offends against your customs?"

"We tie his hands and he receives nothing to eat for a few days or weeks. But such things are rare."

We had been together for ten days when the old man finally said that he had to leave us because he no longer knew the way. He had been told that within three or four days we should reach the river we were aiming for. He wished us luck and left us, our last friend. Our final link with the world was broken.

"Onward, by compass!" became our motto. We had often used the compass in the past, but from this moment it became our best friend. We went directly west.[38] Natural obstacles often stood in our way. Our horses were worn out, and sometimes five or six people had to help a horse move forward.

In addition to natural obstacles, we were hindered by more human moral defects, which became a bigger and bigger problem. Conflicts exploded, sometimes coming close to bloodshed. Impatience made people nervous and quarrelsome. But in this depressing atmosphere they still pushed themselves to the limit in a kind of desperate wish for success. With sweating bodies, swelling veins, tight lips, grinding teeth, we went on. It was as though sheer force of will was propelling us forward.

And this force of will conquered everything.

Four days later, we saw shining before us that loveliest and most desirable of rivers, the Vitim.

CHAPTER XI
On the Vitim

*So far, our adventurous way has taken us by land,
but now we continue by river. After many difficulties
we finally reach our Eldorado.*

Our original plan assumed that all our problems would end when we reached the river. What could be easier than building a few rafts to carry us down to a populated area? But reality, as on so many occasions in the past, was not the same: making plans and carrying them out were two quite different matters.

We eyed the apparently tranquil river with curiosity. How strong were its endlessly flowing currents! Wasn't it amazing that new bodies of water constantly replaced the old, as they flowed downstream? What fate did the waters have in store for us?

It turned out that building rafts was no child's play either. It was very difficult to find the right kinds of wood. But an even greater impediment was our constant bickering and hostility. We had no leader whose word carried any authority. The differences in our social background only made the disagreement deeper. Furthermore, there was growing antagonism between the intellectuals and the rest: the closer we came to our destination, the more we heard voices declaring that in the land of the Soviets intellectuals had no rights and workers were the leaders.

Our deteriorating food supply also had a bad effect on our spirits.

Chapter XI — On the Vitim

A noisy dispute erupted over the form of the rafts. As long as there was no raft-building to be done, everyone had been an expert, but when we actually reached the river only one of the Cossacks had a detailed plan. He calculated that we would need seven rafts – four large ones and three small. We planned to take eight horses with us. The rest we would butcher and eat. The food situation was bad: our hope of varying the menu by hunting and fishing remained unrealized. Our famous hunters always had a reason for returning empty-handed.

"No luck today."

"We saw bison tracks, but we dared not follow them far: we were afraid we couldn't make it back."

"You can't catch fish in muddy water."

And, if the water was clear:

"Fish don't come out in water as clear as this."

There was nothing for it but to eat the horses. But whose horse? At once the argument began. Some people regarded their animals as their own pet possessions and had no wish to offer them up to the common good. Finally, the weakest were condemned to slaughter, and that evening we dined on horse meat and rice. Our dinner was certainly exceptionally tasty. Was this because we were hungry or because the horse meat was good?

Next morning, we looked around for a convenient spot for building the rafts and for suitable trees. In the immediate vicinity we found neither. Only at a distance of a mile or two did we discover enough dry trees. At this point it dawned on us just how superficial our knowledge was, in fact how poor human powers of observation are in general.

There are things we see a thousand times a day, but if someone asked us to describe them in detail, it would turn out that we weren't really familiar with them at all. For example, no one knew how to tie the logs of a raft together. When the Cossack proposed that we use willow branches, lots of people disagreed.

"You want us to risk our lives with a bunch of flimsy twigs?" cried Big Mouth.

"In my entire life, I've never seen anything tied together that way," said the domestic servant. "We need crossbeams or wooden pins."

The Cossack asserted that his was the only method likely to produce good and reliable results, but in vain. Two groups, each of three people, broke off and set to work on their own. Only after they realized they were making no progress did they rejoin the rest.

Soon the frameworks of the rafts were complete and only the oars were lacking – at which point mere chance prevented us from losing everything.

We had pulled the rafts to the river bank and held them in place with stones. During the night the water in the river rose, and the rising current carried our half-ready rafts away. In the course of my story I have frequently quoted our idealistic lawyer. He was a man who lived an intense imaginative life but was extremely clumsy in ordinary matters, so that he was a constant target for our jokes.

The sun was rising when the lawyer, deep in meditation, quite by chance noticed the rafts floating away through the morning mist.

"The river's got our rafts!" he screamed out, plunging into the icy water to seize hold of them and oblivious to the sharp stones wounding his feet. His cries of alarm woke the rest of us and, moments later, half asleep, we were all in the water. We succeeded in recapturing seven rafts; the eighth continued to float away and only our idealist had the courage to struggle to retain it.[39] A desperate battle ensued between man and water, reminiscent of the Victor Hugo novel in which a seaman lashes a loose cannon down in a hurricane.[40]

On that occasion and on this, human strength won out.

We had no medal to give him; we could only silently admire his heroism.

Chapter XI — On the Vitim

Feverishly we began to prepare the oars. Meanwhile, day after day our food supply increased. We ate horse meat in abundance, chiefly roasted, though it did not taste very good without salt. But we slaughtered a further horse because we had room for only eight on our rafts.

As we understood it, there were people living along the lower reaches of the river. So our goal was to reach that area in good order. The overburdened rafts were pushed slightly under the water with the weight of their loads, and we took the thick oars in our hands only with a certain nervousness. In fact, we had traveled no more than an hour on the rafts when a distant thunder reached our ears. It grew steadily louder.

What was the cause of such noise? Rapids? A waterfall? We were frozen with fear at the thought. The rafts moved faster; the hills surrounding us grew higher and the river narrower. As the river curved, the pent-up water increased its roaring and waves a foot or two in height appeared. The horses stood trembling on the rafts while we, wielding the oars with superhuman strength, tried to fend off the rocks. Despite our efforts, two rafts that we had lashed together were thrown on to a rock and their connection broke. The men and horses were terrified. As the men hung struggling to the logs, the horses jumped into the water and swam ashore. For a minute or two this perilous situation continued. With the help of the other rafts we finally succeeded in bringing all the rafts to shore. We lost only a few things.

But this episode essentially changed the general opinion. Up to now, everyone had insisted on bringing the horses with us, but now the majority said that it was the horses that had caused the entire problem and that they should be released into the forest. We decided to free five of them and take only three with us. Four people disagreed with the decision and ended up remaining in the forest with the horses. They demanded their share of the provisions and announced their intention to continue the journey on horseback. We tried in vain to persuade them and finally went on our way without them, and without the five horses.

We lived through many dangers in the next several days. One minute an oar broke, and the next a raft got caught on a sand bank so that even with the help of the horses we could not get it back into the water. Our constant fear was waterfalls. Every time we heard thundering in the distance and listened to its approach, we broke out in a cold sweat. This frenzied gallop over the raging torrent of an unknown river was terrifying, with the river thundering between rocks and rounding sudden bends, each bend threatening us with some new and unexpected peril. How long would it be before we fell into the foaming depths and were torn apart by the sharp rocks? To give a sense of our condition, we lived and traveled on the river for a full week, and never actually washed... Later the river broadened, the stream flowed smoothly, and the sun shone on the rippling waves. On the banks we saw signs of human settlement.[41]

Finally! People! The first we came upon were mining for gold. With much emotion they beheld the rafts that delivered these unknown travelers. Their provisions consisted of milk products and gold, and provided a good opportunity for barter. Even for a box of matches they were willing to give us small amounts of gold. We stayed with them for a few days and then, in populated territory, continued our journey.

Chapter XI — On the Vitim

And so our travels, our robinsonade, *came to an end. Unfortunately, out there in the forest, I had no companion like Crusoe's Friday. My main helpers were an unquenchable desire to return home, and the easy equanimity that comes to a healthy person leading a wandering life – a readiness to sigh and curse if things go badly, but to laugh heartily when they get better. And not to worry about what will happen tomorrow.*

Now, home again and turning it all over in my mind – much suffering and little joy – I find that it has all blended into memory, suffering and joy together. And, strangely but fortunately, every memory always has its beautiful side...

APPENDIX 1:
Who are the Orochen?

The author uses the term "Aracono" to describe the people whom he and his companions meet in the forest. Evidently they described themselves, and were known as, Orochons, the most common way of representing their name at the time. According to Radó, writing seventy years ago (1928: 597-98), "The native population of the Far East is divided into two ethnographic groups sharply differing from each other: the pale-Asiatics and the Manchuro-Tungusian.... The Manchuro-Tunguses have entirely spread themselves along the inner areas of the eastern extremity of the Asiatic Continent." Radó mentions four Manchu tribes, namely "the Manchus proper, the golden hordes, the Ulches and the Udekhs," and four Tunguse tribes, "the Tunguses proper, the Lamutes, the Orochenest, and the Manegres," and explains that "the Tunguses on the whole are deer-breeders."

The community whom the author met were in fact, in today's parlance, members of the Evenk people. "Formerly," says Taksami (1990: 26), "they called themselves the Tungus, but local groups were to be found with individual names: the Orochens in Transbaikalia and the Upper Amur, the Biryars in the Bureya basin and the Manegrs in the Zeya basin." (see our earlier quotation from Radó). In short, the term "Orochen" or "Arachon" is, or was, primarily a local descriptor of Evenks. Today the Evenks appear to be the most numerous of the Manchu-Tungus peoples living in Russia. Census figures (which of course depend upon self-identification and self-assessment and should therefore be used with caution) indicate that there are 28,000 Evenks, of whom about half speak the language (Sunik and Bulatova 1990: 104-105). At least until the collapse of the Soviet Union, Evenk was taught in some schools and there were radio broadcasts and a weekly newspaper.

While it was once customary to make a distinction between Manchu languages and Tungusic languages, and hence between the two ethnic groups, most modern scholars put them in a single Manchu-Tungusic or Tungusic category, consisting of the Evenks (or Ewenki), Evens (or Ewens), Negidals, Nanais, Ulchis, Orokis, Orochis and Udegeys. According to Taksami (1990: 26), "These peoples are scattered over a vast expanse stretching from the Yenisey [east of the Urals] to the Pacific and from the Arctic coast to the southern border." Actually they extend also beyond the border, well into Northern China (see Skorik 1990: 52-53).

The Manchu-Tungus peoples have historically focused on one of three subsistence occupations, the so-called "Northern triad": hunting, fishing, and reindeer-herding, depending on their location and traditions. The northern Evenks have tended to favor herding, and the southern Evenks hunting (Sansone 1980: 47). The author's group probably drove their herds up the Olekma valley from the northern plains to graze in the summer months. Although the northern Evenks are now far less nomadic than they were, reindeer-herding remains a major occupation and is an important element in the economy of many indigenous communities in the northeast. It is estimated that throughout northern Russia there are 2,300,000 head of reindeer (Taksami 1990: 29).

South of the border live the Oroqens, a people closely related to, if not identical with, the Evenks, and, of course, bearing a name very similar to that of the group the author meets in the forest. As southern Evenks, their economy is based primarily on hunting. Until the nineteenth century they used reindeer for transportation and for hunting, but when disease destroyed the reindeer in the area, they switched to horses. The Oroqens in turn are related to the Manchu, whose Manchu-Tungus language has died out but who constitute a large ethnic group of some two and a half million people (at least as the Chinese define their ethnicity). On the Oroqens, see Qui Pu 1983.

In visiting these forest people, the author and his companions experienced a way of life that was already threatened by the march of western ideas and ways of living, and by the development of Siberia. "By the time of the Russian Revolution and Civil War," writes Forsyth (1992: 249), "the Tungus, the most widely dispersed of all the native peoples of Siberia, were also among the most demoralised.... Because of their cultural conservatism and nomadic way of life they were an easy prey for their more aggressive neighbours, whether Russians, Buryats [from the Lake Baikal region], or Yakuts [from the area northeast of Ksenievka], and although some of the Reindeer Tungus of the taiga succeeded in maintaining their traditional way of life by keeping themselves apart, many had lost their independence and become hired labourers."

During the Civil War, the Tungus kept a low profile and were not involved in the struggle to the extent that some of the other indigenous peoples were. "Even if the Tungus did attempt to keep out of the way in the taiga," Forsyth points out (1992: 251), "their small isolated bands were extremely vulnerable to predation by guerilla groups of whatever political persuasion, and in many cases their small herds of reindeer were badly depleted by the commandeering of animals for transport and food. Some Tungus helped the Russian anti-White partisans in their traditional role of pathfinders."

Of all the Siberian peoples, Forsyth suggests (1992: 253), "the Ewenki and Ewen Tungus with their mobile way of life, absence of hierarchical organisation or fixed tribal territory, and traditions of egalitarianism in the distribution of hunting spoils, were perhaps the nation least capable of adapting, or being moulded, to the social preconceptions of the Russian communists." Efforts to collectivize the Evenki in the 1930s essentially failed, though not before a great deal of damage was done to the fabric of their society. Today (see Forsyth, 1992: 381-85), there are still a few Evenki who maintain aspects of their nomadic existence, and their traditions have persisted in part because of the sheer inaccessibility of their favored grazing areas.

It is worth pointing out that there is considerable confusion and uncertainty in the literature concerning the precise identity of the various peoples making up the Manchu-Tungusic group. Although they have been quite extensively studied, there is disagreement on how to name them and how to distinguish among them. Several of the names used for individual peoples essentially reflect local lexical variations in the descriptors that they use to identify themselves. Thus the terms Orochi, Oroki, and Orochen all seem to mean "reindeer people" – as our author mentions in connection with the Orochen (see Majewicz 1989, on the Oroki) – but the three groups occupy (or occupied) different areas in the Lower Amur, on Sakhalin, and in the Upper Amur respectively and may or may not be considered wholly separate peoples. The term Nanai means "local people," and sometimes the Orochi call themselves Nanai, but so do the Nanai.... In short, everything depends on what question is asked. In this as in so many other matters relating to ethnic identity, languages and customs display a certain continuum from community to community and linguistic and cultural boundaries are hard to draw.

References

Collis, Dirmid R. F., ed. 1990. *Arctic Languages: An Awakening.* Paris: Unesco.

Forsyth, James. 1992. *A History of the Peoples of Siberia.* Cambridge: Cambridge University Press.

Majewicz, Alfred E. 1989. The Oroks: Past and Present. In Alan Wood and R.A.French, ed. *The Development of Siberia: People and Resources.* New York: St. Martin's Press. 124-146.

Qui Pu. 1983. *The Oroqens, China's Nomadic Hunters.* Beijing: Foreign Languages Press.

Radó, A. 1928. *Guide-Book to the Soviet Union.* New York: International Publishers.

Sansone, Vito. 1980. *Siberia: Epic of the Century.* Moscow: Progress Publishers.

Skorik, Piotr. Social Functions of the Soviet Northern People's Languages. In Collis 1990: 77-82.

Sunik, Orest, and Nadezhda Bulatova. Evenk. In Collis 1990: 104-105.

Taksami, Chuner. 1990. Ethnic Groups of the Soviet North. In Collis 1990: 83-91.

APPENDIX 2:
Maps

The author's journey takes him from Khabarovsk, in the Russian Far East, to the River Lena. **Map 1** shows ethnic groups of today, in the area in which the events of the narrative take place. The Orochen (Orochi), Oroqen (Oroki) and Evenks (Evenki) can still be located.

Map 2 (see pages 68-69 and also the book jacket) is a detailed representation of the area in question, taken from the reproduction of a wall map published by Literary Digest in the United States in 1934, the closest I could come to the date of Soros's account. The old railroad line through Harbin, Manchuria, is clearly shown. The newer Amur line runs along the Russian side of the border. Before its completion, travelers could also travel by boat from the point east of Chita where the railroad line reaches the Manchurian border, going down the Amur and disembarking in Khabarovsk, where the Ussuri line would take them south to Vladivostok. The route followed by the author's party in the course of the book is indicated. The double line refers to the portion of the journey covered in Maps 3-6.

Map 3 shows the route followed from Ksenievka, to the south, up to Itaka (see notes 22 and 27). From here, the party probably made its way up the valley to the northwest, then west across the mountains to the headwaters of the Inacha, which flows north to the Olekma (see **Map 4**, and note 30). The area immediately north of the Olekma (in the center of Map 4) may well have been the place in which the party met the Orochen (note 35).

Appendix 2 *Map 1*

Map 1: Ethnic groups today in the area of Soros' journey

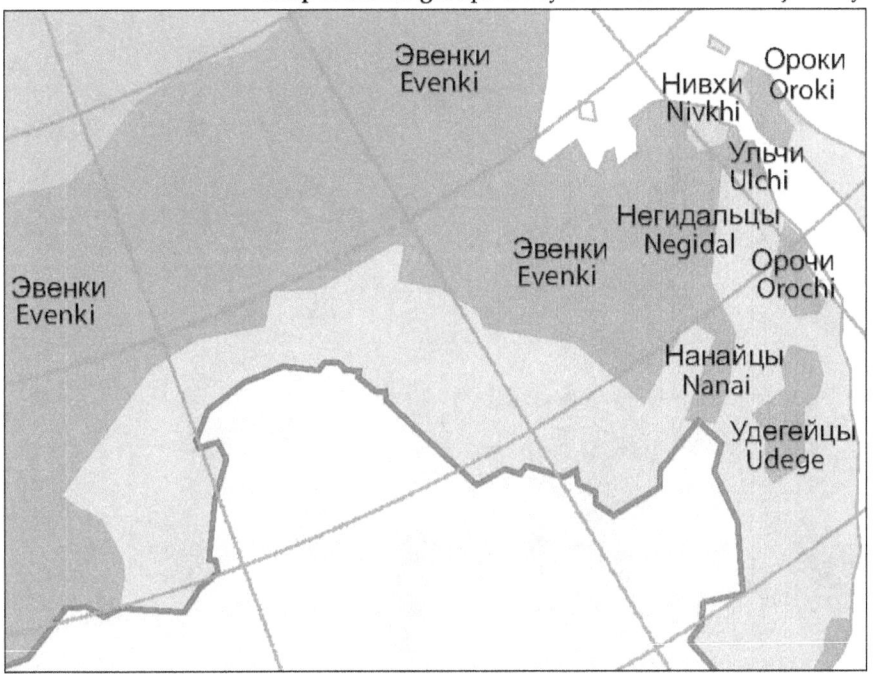

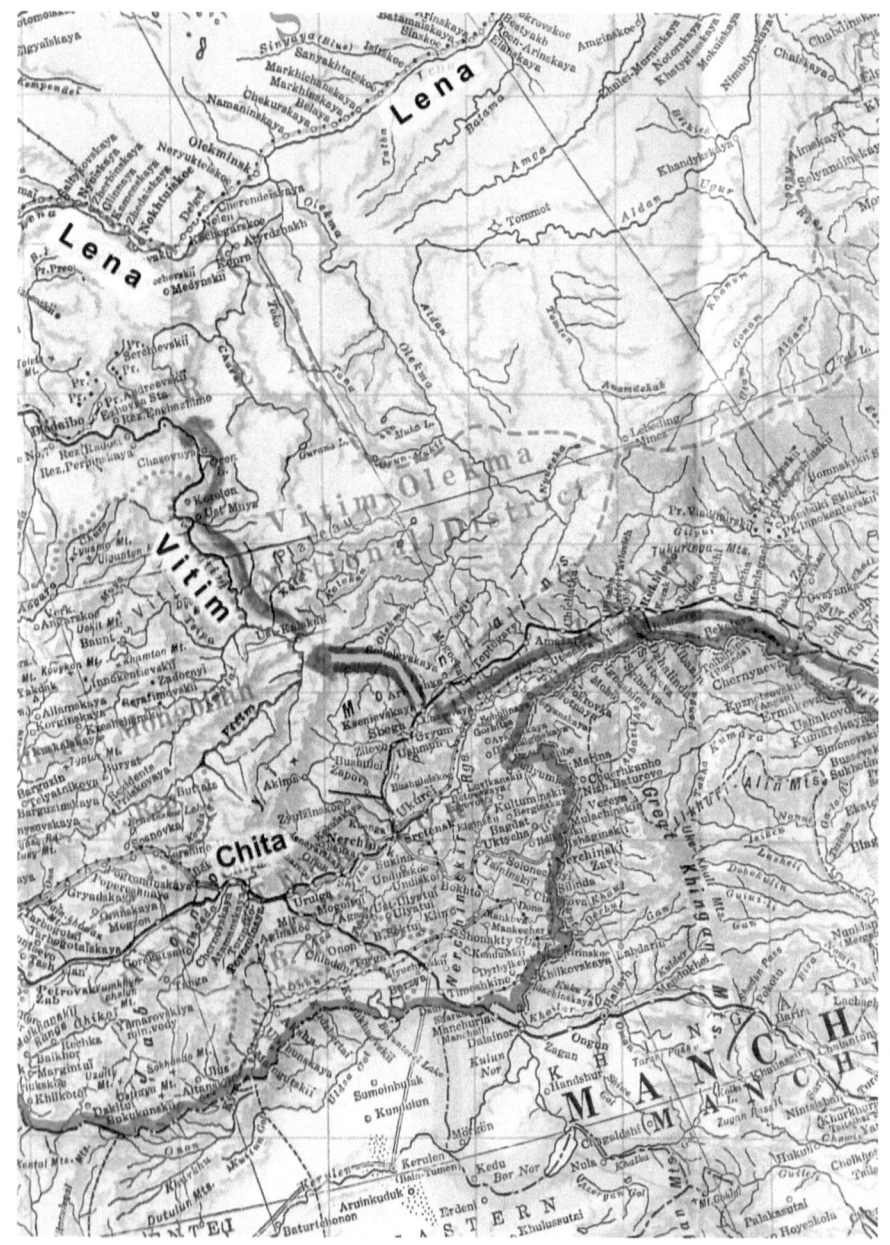

Appendix 2 *Map 2*

Map 2: The route followed by the author's party in the course of the book

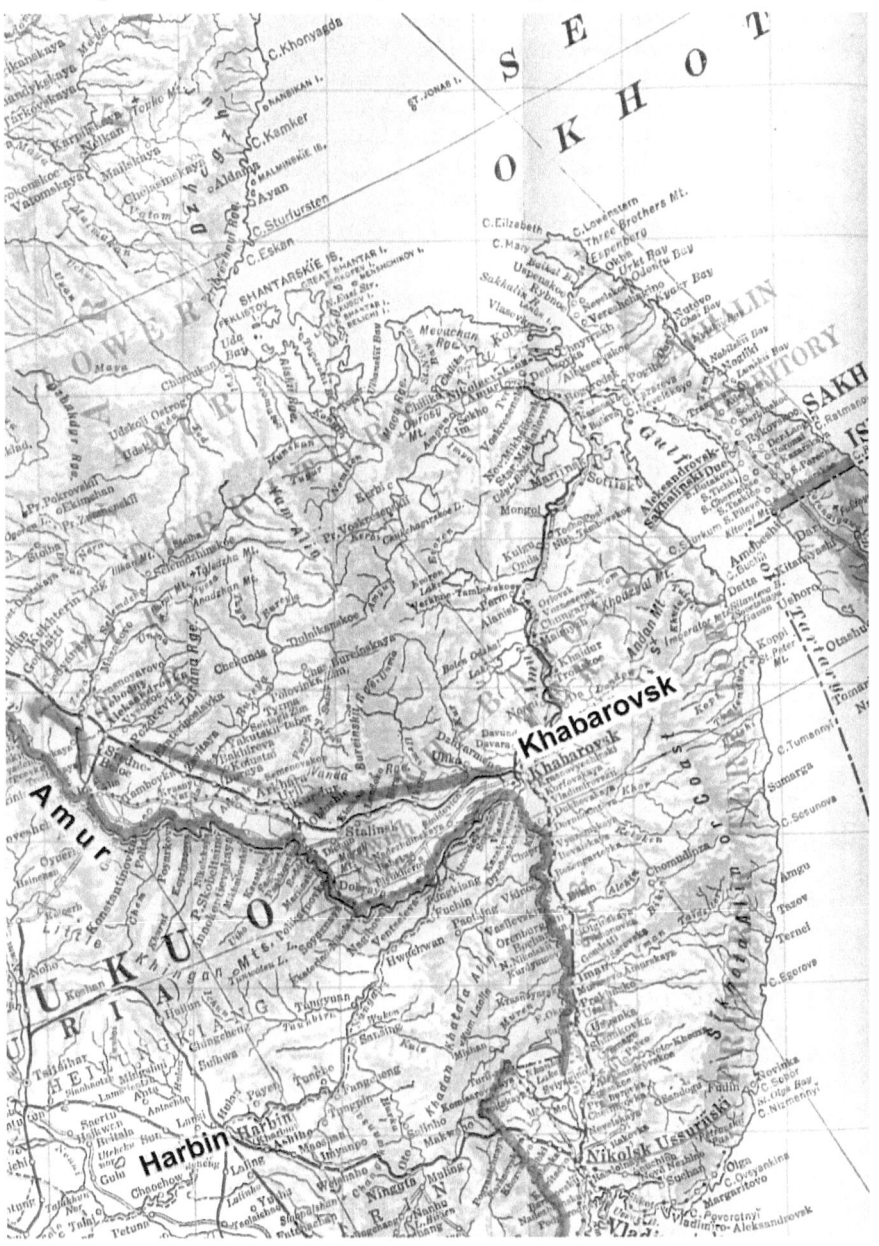

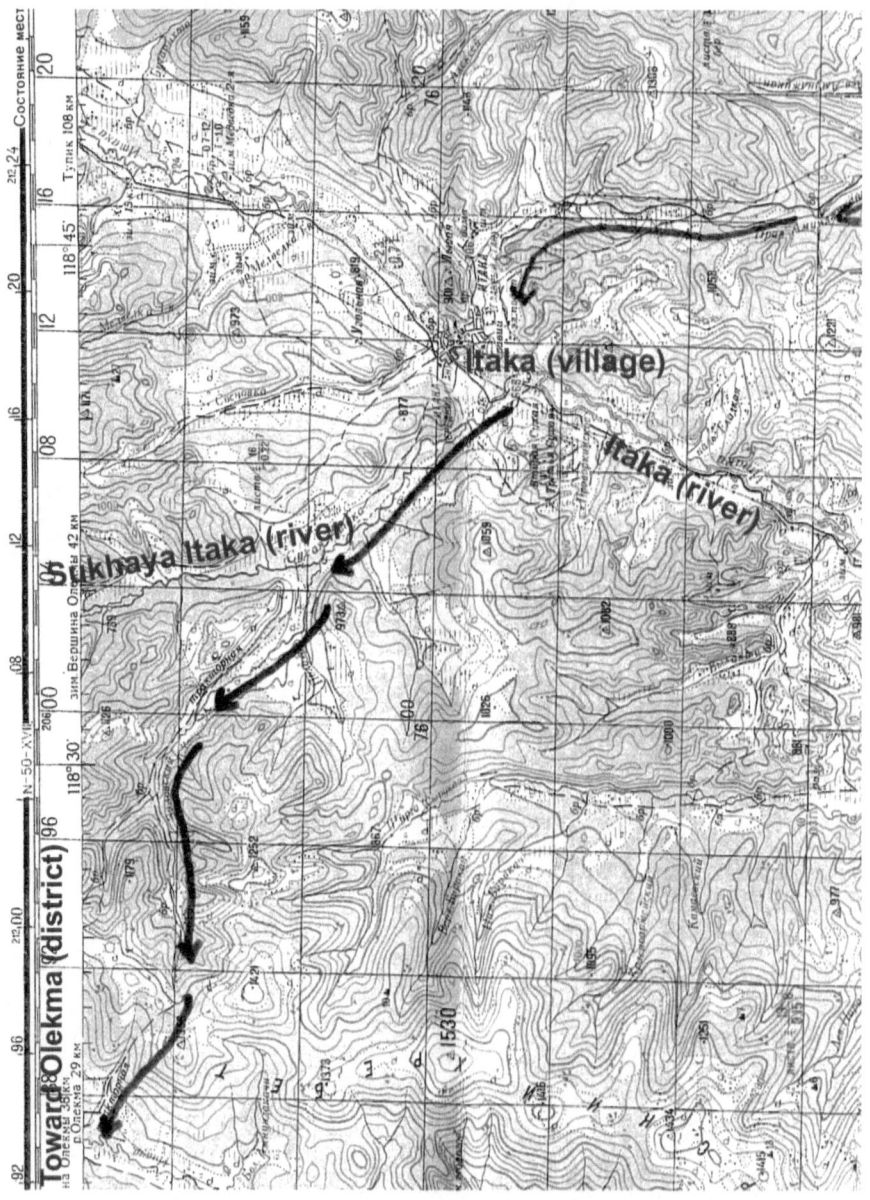

Map 3: From Ksenievka to Itaka

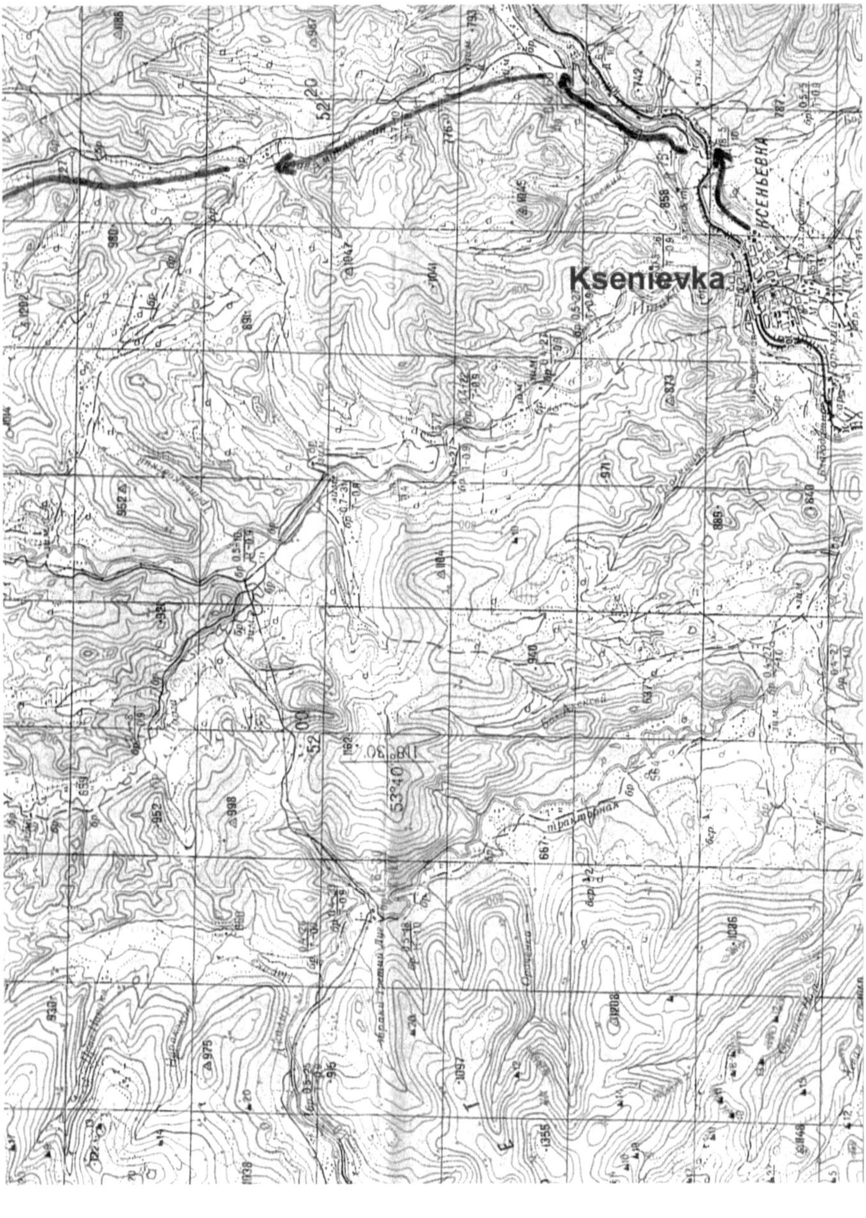

Map 4: Along the rivers Inacha, Olekma, and Veneger

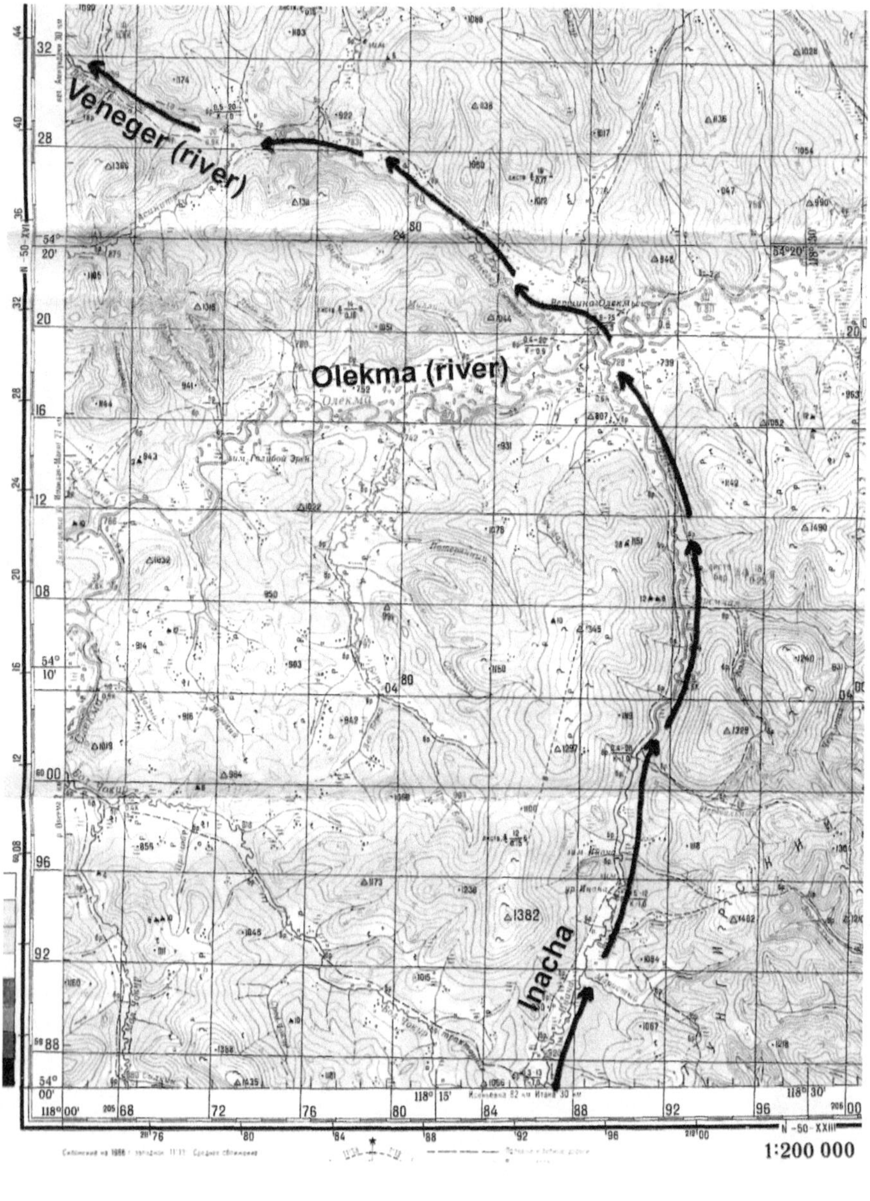

Appendix 2   *Map 4*

After crossing the Olekma, the party headed north and west, up the Veneger, probably then passing south of Mount Veneger, on the eastern edge of **Map 5** (note 36). They probably followed the Nercha for a short distance and then cut across to the Dzhilinda (**Map 5**). Leaving their Orochen guide behind, and climbing the slopes to the west of the Dzhilinda, they would have marched west to the Vitim (**Map 6**, and note 38). Reaching the river, they then headed down the Vitim, northwards, by raft (note 41).

Maps 3-6 are taken from a detailed survey of the entire Soviet Union prepared by Soviet cartographers from the 1940s on. Their original scale was 1: 200,000 (two kilometers per centimeter). The maps were acquired by the Yale University Library in 1990. Different sheets show different dates of revision, but most were revised in the 1980s.

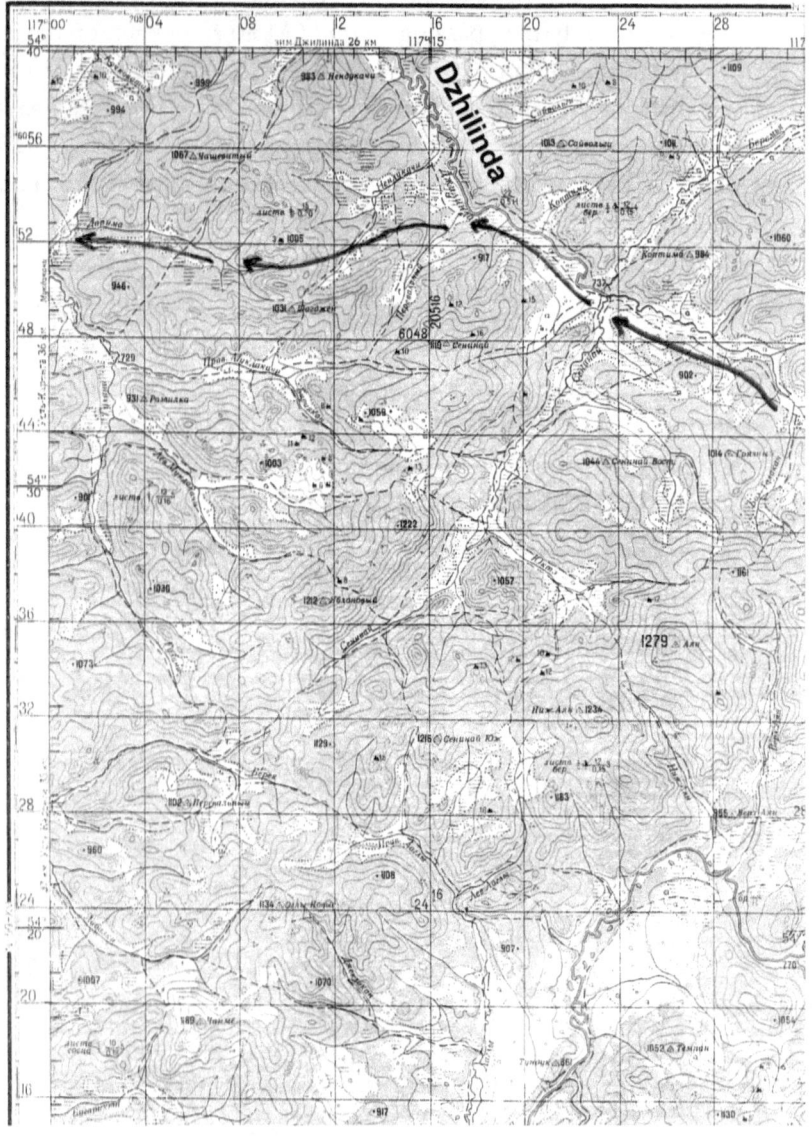

Appendix 2   *Map 5*

Map 5: From Mount Veneger to the Dshilinda river

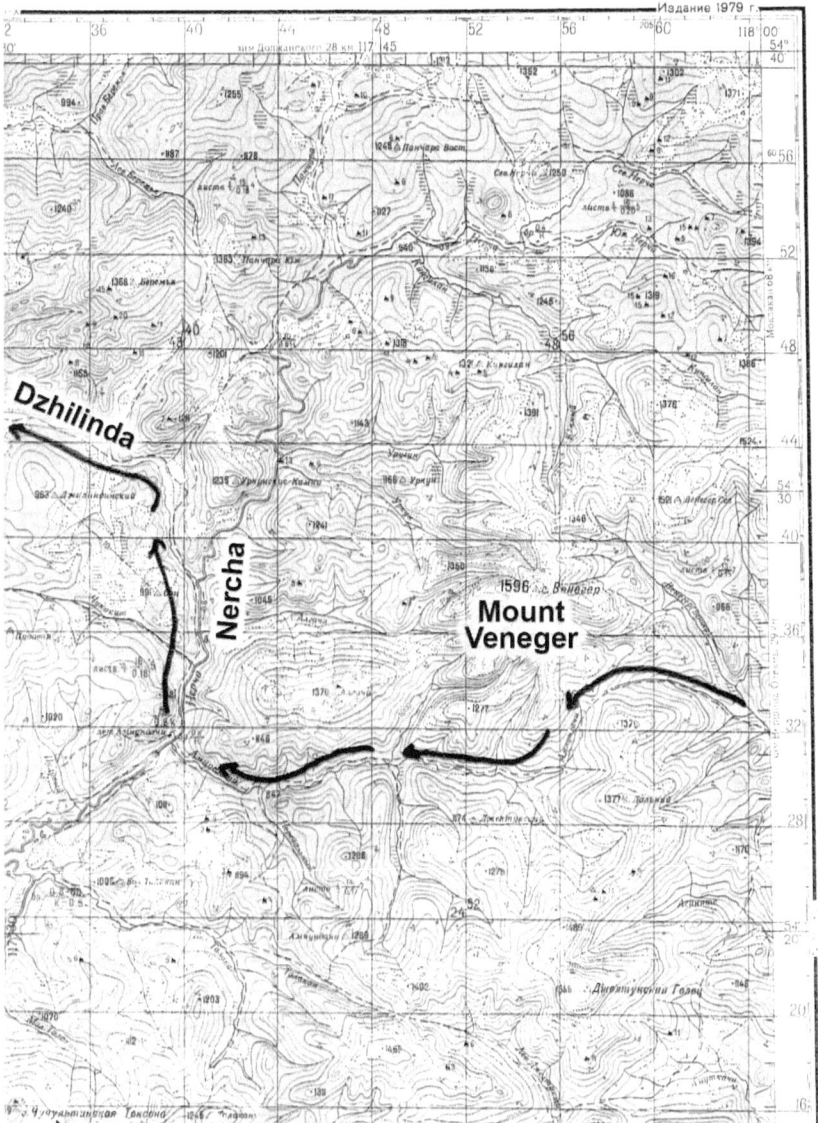

Map 6: Along the Vitim river

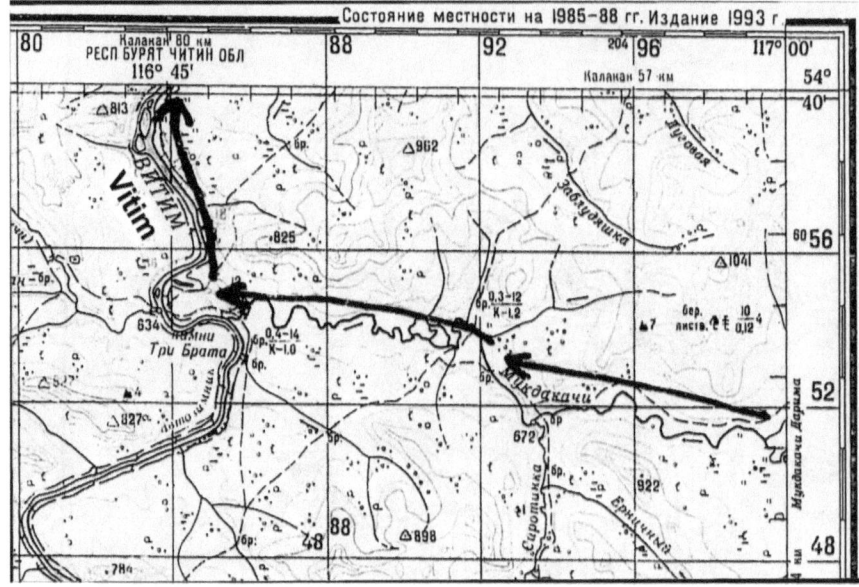

Notes

1. A guidebook from the 1920s (in less than perfect English) describes Khabarovsk, situated 3372 kilometers east of Irkutsk by rail, as the "administrative and economic centre of the Far East Region, situated on the right bank of the river Amur, at the mouth of the river Ussuri. The location of Khabarovsk in the centre of the district, at the junction of the Amur and Ussuri railways, on the water-way of the rivers Amur and Ussuri, makes it the most important town of the Far East. The trade of Khabarovsk is mainly of importing nature…. After the completion of the Amur Railway (to Karimskaya), Khabarovsk became the main transhipping [sic] point for cargoes, coming from Sungari (Manchuria), the upper and lower Amir and over the railways." A.Radó, *Guide-Book to the Soviet Union* (New York: International Publishers, 1928), p. 607. The original Trans-Siberian Railway did not touch Khabarovsk. Begun in 1892, the Railway ran southeast from Irkutsk through Manchurian territory by way of Harbin to Vladivostok, the most direct route. The need to keep this route open led to friction with China and Japan, and the Amur railway, skirting Manchuria to the north, was constructed through Khabarovsk. So the development of Khabarovsk as an important city was a very recent phenomenon.

2. "None of the Western powers knew what their aims were in Siberia; but neither did any of them want to be left out. Under the pretext of guarding Allied stores and keeping the Trans-Siberian Railway open, Western troops were landed in Vladivostok. The British were the first to arrive in early July [1918] with the Middlesex Battalion led by Colonel Ward, the Labour MP for Stoke-on-Trent. It was a

real Dad's Army. Made up of men declared unfit for battle, it was known as the 'Hernia Battalion.' In their smart new khaki uniforms, patently unsuitable for the harsh conditions of Siberia, they soon became an object of ridicule.... French and US troops arrived soon after, followed by the Japanese.... The Western powers wanted a stable government in Siberia in order to resurrect the Russian army and reconstitute the Eastern Front against the Central Powers. But the Japanese, who had ambitions to annex Russia's Far East, wanted, on the contrary, instability.... Never have the taxes of the Western democracies been so criminally wasted." Orlando Figes, *A People's Tragedy: The Russian Revolution 1891-1924* (New York: Penguin Books, 1998), p. 651. Of course, there are other views, among them those of Col. John Ward himself: see his account, *With the "Die-Hards" in Siberia* (New York: Doran, 1920). Ward tells us that the troops arrived in August, not July. The Americans followed in September, the French in November.

3. One of the ostensible reasons for Allied intervention in Siberia was a fear, much exaggerated as it turned out, of Austro-Hungarian and German collaboration with the Bolsheviks. The Russians captured huge numbers of prisoners in the course of the war – some two million in all; and as early as 1918 numbers of Germans, Austrians and Hungarians began to turn up in the Red Army. Following the Treaty of Brest-Litovsk, the Germans took steps to repatriate as many of their soldiers as possible, including those fighting for the Reds. The Austrians and Hungarians had no one to serve as their advocate and were left moldering in various parts of Russia. Hardly surprisingly, these prisoners looked for ways out. Some were indeed captured several times over, rather than merely changing hands among the Allies. An Allied raid on Blagoveshchensk on September 20, 1918, for example, turned up a number of Germans, Austrians and Hungarians in arms in support of the partisans. On Allied fears, see Sophia Rogoski Petzel, *American Intervention in Siberia 1918-1920*, dissertation, University of Pennsylvania, Philadelphia, 1946.

4   The commander of the American Expeditionary Force in Siberia throughout its service there, from 1918 to April 1920, was in fact General William S. Graves (1865-1940), who subsequently wrote about his experience in *America's Siberian Adventure* (New York, 1931). Our author is presumably referring to Colonel Charles H. Morrow, commander of two battalions of the 27th Infantry, whose headquarters were at Khabarovsk from the time of the arrival of the Americans in early September 1918 until April 1919, when he and his two thousand men were moved to the Lake Baikal area. Morrow had a reputation as a fearless and strong-willed individual and he had a number of collisions with Grigoriy Semenov, the Cossack leader. See Clarence A. Manning, *The Siberian Fiasco* (New York: Library Publishers, 1952), and Robert Maddox, *The Unknown War with Russia* (San Rafael: Presidio Press, 1977). Maddox (p. 73) quotes one of Morrow's fellow officers to the effect that the Japanese regarded Morrow "as a sort of bomb with the fuse already lighted."

5   General Maurice Janin, formerly head of the French military mission in Russia. On his role as French commander see J. Rouquerol, *L'Aventure de l'Amiral Koltchak*, Paris: Payot, 1929.

6   Admiral Alexander Kolchak, leader of the White Army, abandoned Omsk on November 14, 1919, in the face of the Red Army's advance, with the aim of establishing his government at Irkutsk. Along the way, he resigned his command, and was brought to Irkutsk by Czecho-Slovak troops in the expectation that he would be handed over to the Allies. Irkutsk, meanwhile, had come largely under the control of the Bolsheviks, and the Czechs, wishing to barter a safe passage home, turned him over to them. He was executed in February 1920.

7   American withdrawal began in January 1920, when troops were pulled back from the Lake Baikal region. By April 1920, all American troops had left.

8   As we have seen (above), the city was already largely in the hands of the Bolsheviks.

9   Alexandre Dumas' novel (1844) describes a particularly dramatic escape from imprisonment by its hero, Edmond Dantès.

10 Presumably the Amur.

11 "By the height of the Kolchak offensive, whole areas of the Siberian rear were engulfed by peasant revolts. This partisan movement could not really be described as Bolshevik, as it was later by Soviet historians, although Bolshevik activists, usually in a united front with the Anarchists and Left SRs [members of the Socialist Revolutionary Party], often played a major role in it. It was rather a vast peasant war against the Omsk regime. Sometimes the local peasant chieftains were somewhat confused as to what they were fighting for." Figes, *A People's Tragedy*, p. 657.

12 "Blagoveschensk, centre of the Amur district, a town with 57 000 inhabitants. It is situated at the conflux of the navigable rivers Amur and Zea. A large commercial port." Radó, *Guide-Book*, p. 606. In 1900 the city was the scene of a major massacre of Chinese residents by the Cossacks in retaliation for the murders of Europeans in China during the Boxer Rebellion (Bryn Thomas, *Trans-Siberian Handbook*, Hindhead, Surrey: Trailblazer, 1997, p. 349). The city was located on a branch of the Amur railway, extending southwards from Bochkarevo some 109 kilometers. So evidently the next leg of the journey began by returning to Bochkarevo and then heading west.

13 Zabaykalskiy is the final Russian stop on the old Trans-Siberian Railway, which cut through China (Manchuria) to Vladivostok. It lies close to the point where the borders of Mongolia, China and Russia come together.

14 The train must have stopped somewhere in the vicinity of Amazar or Mogocha, a particularly inhospitable mountainous region.

15 Ksenievskaya, or Ksenievka, is almost 1000 kilometers west of Bochkarevo, so on this leg of the journey rather more than 1000 kilometers were covered. Ksenievskaya was a tiny community linked with the outside world only by the railroad. Even today it remains extremely isolated, and its economy revolves around logging and mining. Situated in a small marshy valley between the Eastern Yablonovy mountains to the north and south, with peaks rising to around 3000 feet, it stands on the south bank of the Cherniy Uryum River, where the Imaka River joins it from the north. The railroad line runs northeast/southwest at this point, paralleling the river.

16 The climate in this region was, and is, horrendous. Mogocha, slightly to the east of Ksenievka, is described by Bryn Thomas (*Trans-Siberian Handbook*, p. 344) as "probably the harshest place to live" on the Trans-Siberian Railway "because of the permafrost and the summer sun.". His description of the local circumstances gives a good idea of what life in Ksenievka must have been like as well: "In winter the top 10 centimeters of Earth that thawed in the summer freezes over again in temperatures as low as -60° (-87°F), killing all but the hardiest plants, while the summer sun singes most shoots."

17 Vito Sansone (*Siberia: Epic of the Century*. Moscow: Progress Publishers, 1980, p. 191) quotes a Yakut herdsman from somewhat further north who describes the change of seasons in strikingly similar fashion: "Our land is a region of twilight. On November 15 or 16 the sun disappears behind the mountains and we don't see it again until January 27. The night lasts for 10 weeks. In summer, on the other hand, the day lasts two months without a break…. Summer begins unexpectedly…. On June 8 the forest is as black as you see it now. The next day buds begin to open on the trees and the taiga is covered with a soft yellow. By June 10 the entire forest is green. The grass in the fields is already high, with the most brilliant flowers amid it; the air smells of pine, and wild ducks, geese, black-cock and ptarmigan begin building nests. The animals of the taiga come

out of their burrows and lairs and fish frisk in the lakes. Nature is in motion and everywhere the air is filled with sound. Everything is in a hurry, everything is gripped by an indescribable haste.... Winter begins just as unexpectedly. On August 15 the taiga is still green; on August 18 it becomes yellowish, on August 19 it is red and after that it immediately becomes dark. Night frosts begin on August 20." The author and his party were at a latitude about the same as Hudson's Bay and southern Alaska.

18 According to Radó, *Guide-Book*, pp. 597-98, writing a few years later, the total population of the Russian Far East "is 1,667,000 souls, 72.8% of this being the rural population. The Far East is very poorly and unequably populated. The bulk of the vast area of the country is deserted, and is populated only in the valleys of the rivers and in the vicinity of the railways. The Russians form 54.4% of the population, the Ukrainians 22.1% and the White-Russians 1.9%, the Coreans 6.9% and the Chinese 3.2%, while all the other minor nationalities compose only 6.5%." On the Orochen, see our Appendix.

19 Presumably the decision to reach the Lena by way of the Vitim obviated the need to go as far to the north-east as Yakutsk: the travelers could pick up the steamship, if the line still existed, as it made its way up the Lena past the point where the Vitim flowed into it. If their intention had been to reach Yakutsk, they could have followed the Olekma northwards rather than cutting across the mountains westwards to the Vitim.

20 I have been unsuccessful in identifying the meaning of the abbreviation or in finding any additional information on Shilov.

21 One of the announced goals of the allied presence in eastern Siberia was to control the Trans-Siberian Railway. The Japanese, British and Americans signed an understanding on January 9, 1919, to establish an Interallied Railway Agreement to keep the line open (see Brune, *Chronological History*; Manning, *Siberian Fiasco*, pp. 114-122). This arrangement continued until early 1920. Evidently by the time

that we are now dealing with – the spring of 1920 – this control had slipped and partisans had taken over at various points along the line. All of the Allies had either left or were about to leave, with the exception of the Japanese. On the use of railroad cars as living quarters, Roquerol, *L'Aventure*, p. 62, has some interesting observations. He points out that General Janin spent three months in a railroad car from the time of his arrival in Vladivostok to the time of his arrival in the Lake Baikal region, and then a further five and a half months going back. Railroad cars were in fact the usual living quarters for military commanders, who moved from place to place by hitching their cars on to passing trains.

22 Today, there is a road leading north from Ksenievka to Itaka, and a road running southeast. Several other seasonal roads run up the valleys extending to the north of Ksenievka, and the group might have followed any of these valleys. However, two factors point particularly to the Itaka route. First is the need for a "special train" to take the group to a point slightly northeast of Ksenievka: the other most likely route goes due north from Ksenievka and would not have necessitated a train ride. The only other possibility is that the party took the train in a southwesterly direction, to one of the valleys in that area. If they did, they would ultimately have found themselves obliged to cross a considerable river that runs towards the south, the Nerchuzan or Nercha. There is no mention of this river anywhere in the text. Secondly, given that the Japanese were still active in the area south of Ksenievka and also in control in the east, the partisans would most likely be interested in routes that would take them northwards out of the range of the Japanese. Perhaps they were interested in reaching the Olekma River, which would open up a line of communication to the north.

23 Modern maps suggest a different picture. Perhaps the marshy areas surrounding parts of the Olekma River were included in the river as it was represented on the map the party had. This would

make the Cherniy Uryum, which for the most part flows through a narrow valley, seem manageable by comparison.

24 "Es irrt der Mensch, so lang er strebt," Man errs as long as he strives, as the Lord puts it in the Prologue in Heaven at the beginning of *Faust*, Part One. This is the closest parallel that we have been able to find in Goethe, after much consultation of concordances and the racking of the memory of numerous specialists in German literature (our particular thanks to Dr. Detlev Blanke, of Berlin). There are several passages in Schiller (rather than Goethe) that bear some resemblance to the sentiments expressed here, but our author's recollection was probably simply imprecise.

25 A common way of proceeding. Many Austrians and Hungarians coming out of prisoner-of-war camps were pressed into service by either the Reds or the Whites.

26 Probably at Sbega, where the Cherniy Uryum and the Belyts Uryum join to form the Chernaya River, which flows in turn into the Shilka River, a tributary of the Amur. At Sbega the railroad crosses the Cherniy Uryum as it heads west towards Chita. Sbega is in fact only about twenty-five miles southwest of Ksenievka, rather than the hundred miles mentioned by the author. The course of the two rivers is such that there must have been a bridge there also in the author's time.

27 The author's text gives only the most sketchy of information about the route followed by the group, but numbers of topographical details can be inferred from the text, and in any case an examination of detailed maps of the area makes it clear that the choice of routes was quite limited. The valleys between the mountains here run essentially north-south, and recent maps show that only one of these valleys has a road running through it. Today, about five miles northeast of Ksenievka there is a bridge across the river carrying a road that leads to the town of Itaka, some twenty-five miles to the

north. The railroad follows the southern bank of the river. If we accept the proposition that our party would have sought out the most likely crossing place and that modern road-builders would do the same, we can surmise that this was the place where the party crossed the river. It is distant enough from Ksenievka – some three miles – to have required the "special train" mentioned in the previous chapter to carry equipment for building the bridge. The present-day road to Itaka follows the northern bank of the river for a while, through what appears to be marshy land. It then turns north, continuing up a marshy valley for several miles. The fact that the commander specified that the group would be responsible for twenty-five miles of road supports the assumption that he had in mind reaching what is now Itaka.

28 Further support for the view that the route was the same as that now followed by the road to Itaka. There is no mention of following a river: the road goes over mountains and through valleys according to the text.

29 Presumably the telegraph wires along the railroad.

30 The watershed between the Cherniy Uryum (which ultimately flows south towards the Pacific Ocean) and the Olekma, which flows north towards the Arctic Ocean, is rather more than ten miles distant from Itaka. This would suggest that we might be wrong in assuming that the route led through what is now Itaka. Conceivably the party followed one of the valleys further to the west. However, even in that area there is no place that entirely fits the distances mentioned by the author. I am inclined, therefore, to conclude that he was simply mistaken and that initially the group went uphill rather than downhill, following the Sukhaya Imaka, a tributary of the Imaka (which flows past Itaka), and then cut across the mountains to the west to reach the Inacha River, which descends to the Olekma. The Inacha is the most likely candidate for the "stream

that flowed down into the Olekma River," since it extends a long way south into the mountains.

31 If the group followed the Inacha, the distance from Itaka to the Olekma would be some thirty-five miles, which seems about appropriate for a three-day march, given the other indications in the text.

32 The Olekma meanders through a broad valley, descending gradually to the east-northeast. The Inacha joins with it from the south in the middle of a flat plain several miles in extent. To the north, another river, the Veneger, or Venoer, also joins the Olekma. Given the flatness of the area, it would seem very possible that the river would not be particularly deep.

33 On the identity of the forest people, see Appendix 1, "Who are the Orochen?"

34 Such experiences may have reinforced the author's interest in Esperanto when he reached Moscow. During the early Soviet period and the relative cultural freedom at the time, Esperanto acquired considerable popularity. For a history of Esperanto in Russia during this period see Ulrich Lins, *La danĝera lingvo* (Gerlingen, Germany: Bleicher, 1988) and the German version of the same book, *Die gefährliche Sprache* (Gerlingen, Germany: Bleicher, 1988).

35 The confluence of the Inacha, Veneger and Olekma rivers would be a particularly good setting for such a village (or perhaps encampment would be a more suitable term for a nomadic people). In essence the area is a flood plain, where trees would be unlikely to grow in great profusion, and where there would probably be an abundance of grass.

36 From the Olekma, the party could have followed its tributary, the Veneger, northwestwards, then turning westwards across the southern flanks of Mount Veneger, a 4000-foot peak, and then across the headwaters of the Nercha to the headwaters of the Dzhilinda,

which flows northeast, ultimately joining the Vitim, though at a point north of where our party probably did so.

37 "The harsh climate shaped the character, customs, and ways of the people; it formed the psychology of solitude. Life in small communities lost in gloomy forests and the absence of news and striking events bred a taciturn race possessing strong feelings of comradeship and justice. Murder and theft did not exist. Locks were neither used nor useful. Since there were no professional craftsmen each family had to make everything necessary for life and work for itself.... Like other Asian peoples following a nomadic way of life, the Yakuts, Evens, Evenks and Yukaghirs, divided into family groups of several dozen people, wandered unhurriedly with their *yurts* over the taiga and tundra." Sansone, *Siberia*, pp. 161-162.

38 If the party did reach the headwaters of the Dzhilinda, then by turning west they would reach the Vitim at its closest point, where the river turns from an easterly course to flow northwards. The distance would indeed be about appropriate for a march of three or four days. It would involve going over a further range of mountains (the "natural obstacles" to which the author refers) with peaks of about 3000 feet and then following one of the valleys down to the Vitim.

39 Did the author and his companions build seven rafts or eight? Earlier in the chapter there is a reference to seven rafts, four large and three small.

40 Victor Hugo was something of a specialist in human battles against the ocean. Such episodes occur in *The Toilers of the Sea* (*Les Travailleurs de la mer*) and *The Man Who Laughs* (*L'Homme qui rit*). But the author is referring here to Hugo's novel *Ninety-Three* (*Quatre-vingt-treize*) of 1879, in which a cannon breaks loose on the corvette the "Claymore" as it is carrying a fugitive from the French Revolution, the Marquis de Lentenac, traveling incognito, to safety in the Channel Islands. The gunner, who was originally responsible for allow-

ing the cannon to break loose, carries on a huge battle with it, in which he is assisted in the final stages by the Marquis, rising aristocratically to the occasion.

41 The Vitim, on its upper reaches, alternates between relatively level sandy areas and severe drops in altitude. A long stretch of rapids, the Delyun Uran Rapids, was famous for its extent and severity. The lower stretch of the river, from Bodaibo two hundred miles to the town of Vitim, where the Vitim joined the Lena, was calmer. Bodaibo was a major gold-mining center.

The Fairest Judgment
After an Indian fable

by Teo Melas [Tivadar Soros]

Tivadar Soros's tale "The Fairest Judgment," mentioned by George Soros in his preface, appeared in an early issue of Tivadar's journal Literatura Mondo. *Variants of this story are common in the literatures of India, though no definite source has been identified. By way of completeness (in addition to* Crusoes in Siberia *and* Maskerado, *it is his only known other literary venture), we reprint it here in English translation.*

The Fairest Judgment — After an Indian Tale

Ramigan, the great skeptic, whose judgments and sentences were famous from the Yellow Sea to the Tigris and Euphrates, was sitting quietly and in good humor among his disciples.

"Great sage," asked one of them, "your wisdom shines like a torch in the darkness of the jungle. Our souls are thirsty for its light; direct a single beam from it upon us."

The Master, who was accustomed to telling a story to his disciples after a good and abundant evening meal – because storytelling has a favorable influence on the digestion – affably replied:

"Good, I will tell you about my fairest judgment. Listen carefully."

In an Indian village there lived a brahman. He was not excessively wealthy, but he none the less had one special treasure: a daughter fairer than the red of sunrise, more graceful than the lotus flower trembling in the silver beams of the moon. Her body was fresher than the foam of a stream in springtime; in her eyes burned mysterious flames, and amidst her abundant hair was hidden the sweet spirit of jasmine flowers. It was said that Kamadeva flew around her constantly and that he loosed an arrow from his flowery bow at every man who had the courage to approach her. She was called Madhupamanjari because, like bees to a blossomed branch, she drew all men to her with her sweet attraction.

Four young men asked for her hand. But she could not choose among them. Her heart, like a reed in the wind, bent now to one, now to another.

One day, when she was sleeping in the garden, a poisonous serpent bit her, and she died.

Everyone was seized with inexpressible sorrow. Her father died of a tormented heart. Her lovers wept and moaned.

The first lover could not endure life without her. When, in accordance with sacred custom, her body was burned, he threw himself into the flames and perished. His ashes mixed with the ashes of the worshipped girl.

The second made a solemn vow that for the rest of his life he would not move from her adored tomb, but would guard her ashes faithfully.

The third shrugged his shoulders and quietly, as if nothing had happened, went home to his village.

The fourth sought to forget by wandering through the world.

This fourth lover traveled for a long, long time. One day, in the late evening, he came to a small house, and, weary, he asked that he might rest there for the night. The master of the house accepted him hospitably, regaling him with a fine dinner. But it happened that the son of the master, a mischievous child, while running around the table, fell over, and, seizing the edge of the tablecloth, caused all the dishes to fall to the ground. Seeing the broken dishes, the father fell into a fury, and in sudden anger he caught up his son and flung him into the fire. Upon witnessing the cruel death of the child, our wanderer grew extremely indignant. "What cruelty, what abomenation! Not for a moment longer will I remain in the house of such a man!" he cried, and moved to go. "Be calm, my friend," said the master of the house; "nothing terrible has happened." And he took a book, read from it seven magic words, and, behold, the child, alive, jumped cheerfully out of the ashes.

Our wanderer waited impatiently for the night. When night fell, he took the book and stole out of the house. Day and night, without pausing for rest, he rushed along; the beating of his heart, like so many strokes of a whip, drove him home to the tomb of the adored Madhupamanjari.

Arriving at the tomb, he read the seven magic words from the book, and behold! Like Shri, the goddess of love, appearing from the waves of the ocean, Madhupamanjari rose up from the ashes, smiling, and a hundred times more beautiful.

But with her rose up also the young man who had thrown himself in the flames.

And, with shouts of joy, the hitherto motionless guardian of the tomb jumped up, stretching his cramped limbs.

And the rapidly spreading news of the miracle soon caused the fourth young man to arrive.

So, once again, four young men sought the hand of Madhupamanjari. And her heart remained like a reed in the wind. She could not decide.

Finally she said, "Let him who most deserves me have me." And so they came to me to ask my judgment.

"And so? How did you judge her?" the disciples, full of curiosity, asked.

"My wisdom expressed the verdict in this way:

"He who revived the girl is worthy to be her father, because he gave life to her.

"He who threw himself inth the flames is worthy to be her brother, because he was willing to sacrifice himself for her.

"He who guarded her ashes so faithfully is worthy to be her willing slave for evermore.

"And he who shrugged his shoulders and went quietly home is worthy to be her husband. Let him have the girl."

"Great is our master," cried the disciples in unison.

www.ingramcontent.com/pod-product-compliance
Lightning Source LLC
Chambersburg PA
CBHW020358170426
43200CB00005B/214